BLACK CABS
AND
SLEEPING
POLICEMEN

BLACK CABS
AND
SLEEPING
POLICEMEN

BY
HARRY OLIVER

metro

Published by Metro Publishing
an imprint of John Blake Publishing Ltd
3 Bramber Court, 2 Bramber Road,
London W14 9PB, England

www.johnblakepublishing.co.uk

First published in hardback in 2009

ISBN: 978-1-84454-854-5

British Library Cataloguing-in-Publication Data:

A catalogue record for this book is available from the British Library.

Design by www.envydesign.co.uk

Printed in the UK by CPI William Clowes Beccles NR34 7TL

1 3 5 7 9 10 8 6 4 2

© Text copyright Harry Oliver 2009
© Illustrations copyright Mike Mosedale 2009

Papers used by John Blake Publishing are natural, recyclable products made
from wood grown in sustainable forests. The manufacturing processes
conform to the environmental regulations of the country of origin.

Every attempt has been made to contact the relevant copyright-holders,
but some were unobtainable. We would be grateful if the appropriate
people could contact us.

For Bruce

CONTENTS

CONTENTS

ACKNOWLEDGEMENTS

First and foremost, my thanks go to Becky and Jo for their help and advice. Mary Tobin for her efficient editing, and to Allie at Metro for her patience. As always Mike Mosedale has come up with fantastic illustrations – thanks Mike – and Graeme Andrew has once again designed and typeset beautifully.

'Mugging too lah-di-dah for you then?'

INTRODUCTION

The idea for this book was born on a sunny day in August 2008. It was my wife's birthday, and we'd both taken a break from work to take a leisurely amble around London, the place we call home. Walking from Victoria station, we made our way to the river, passing The Tate Britain and then the houses of Parliament. Continuing along the Embankment, we eventually arrived at St Paul's Cathedral and crossed The Millennium Bridge to the Tate Modern on the South Bank. After having a peek at the art gallery's contents, we went for a drink near the Globe Theatre. Sipping our pints, we talked about the day, the places we'd passed, and marvelled at the sheer number of people who'd been doing the same activity as us: looking at things. British things. And then we marvelled at the sheer number of things there had been to look at: the buildings, the taxis, the telephone boxes, even the pints in our hands were all peculiar to Britain, or at least seemed that way. As it so often does, our conversation turned to books. Was the idea of a book on the origins of London icons 'a good one'? Perhaps, but maybe a bit narrow – London's not the only place in Britain, after all. What about a book that considered the origins of the iconic 'things' that defined our richly diverse country as a whole? Now that was more like it.

Within half an hour we'd excitedly made a list of over a hundred items that we'd like to know more about, and two hours later we had three times that number. The ideas kept coming, and we soon realised there was enough for at least two books on the subject. The book you are holding now is the first. As always, my aim was to provide short informative entries that will divert and entertain, and offer the reader food for thought. With a subject as vast as Britishness, the only way to offer anything close to a comprehensive work would be to produce an Encyclopaedia – a lifetime's work. I have endeavoured to provide a range of entries, some nostalgic, some contemporary, and (providing this book proves interesting to readers!) look forward to doing the same in a second volume. There are an endless number of British icons to be celebrated, and I look forward to finding out more.

I am always grateful for suggestions, comments, and corrections from readers, so any Britain buffs should feel free to email my publisher: words@blake.co.uk. Thanks for reading!

CHAPTER ONE
GREAT BRITISH INSTITUTIONS

'Sorry guys...budget cuts!'

GREAT BRITISH INSTITUTIONS

Amnesty International
Demanding 'justice for those whose rights have been violated' is the noble edict of the international non-governmental organisation Amnesty International. Peter Benenson was travelling on the Underground in London on 19 November 1960 when he read about two Portuguese students who'd been sentenced to seven years in prison for some minor offence. Outraged, the labour lawyer founded Amnesty with friend Eric Baker in London in 1961. 'Open your newspaper any day of the week and you will find a story from somewhere of someone being imprisoned, tortured or executed because his opinions or religion are unacceptable to his

government,' he famously wrote in an *Observer* article entitled 'The Forgotten Prisoners'. It marked the launch of 'Appeal for Amnesty, 1961' to mobilise public opinion in defence of 'Prisoners of Conscience'. The appeal was picked up on by several papers worldwide, and that same year Benenson published *Persecution 1961*, a book detailing several cases. His appeal would form the basis of Amnesty International. The first meeting was held in July 1961, with delegates from Belgium, the UK, France, Germany, Ireland, Switzerland and the US. The group decided to establish 'a permanent international movement in defence of freedom of opinion and religion'. The organisation grew and grew, and today Amnesty International has over 2.2 million members, supporters and subscribers in over 150 countries.

Bank of England

The government's finances were in a bit of a pickle when King William and Queen Mary came to the throne in 1688. In 1694, the Scotsman William Paterson proposed to loan them £1.2 million, to be repaid at a rate of 8 per cent per annum, along with an annual service charge of £4,000. In return, the subscribers would be incorporated as the Governor and Company of the Bank of England. Extortionate though it seemed, the authorities didn't have much choice. Thus, the bank began life in Walbrook, London, above the ancient Temple of Mithras (the god of contracts), before moving to its current location on Threadneedle Street in 1734. With 17 clerks and two gatekeepers, the bank acted as the government's banker and debt-manager, as well as taking deposits and issuing bank notes.

BBC

The world's largest broadcasting corporation, the British Broadcasting Corporation, or 'the Beeb' as it is more fondly known, is funded by an annual licence fee to all households who own a working television set. The corporation was founded in 1922 by British and American electrical companies and issued a licence by the Postmaster General, Neville Chamberlain. The first newscast was broadcast from Marconi House to London, and read by the then Director of Programmes, Arthur Burrows. The Beeb was granted a Royal Charter and became publicly funded in 1927, its dictum being to 'be free from both political and commercial influence and answer only to its viewers and listeners'. TV broadcasts, reaching up to 40,000 homes in London, began in 1932 but were suspended throughout the Second

World War. ITV arrived on the scene in 1955, to give the BBC a run for its money. The BBC responded by launching a second channel, BBC 2, though it was delayed by a massive power failure caused by a fire at Battersea Power Station. BBC 2 was the first European station to broadcast regularly in colour, from 1967 onwards. In the Sixties, the radio stations were split into BBC 1, 2, 3 and 4, with the BBC World Service being partly funded by the Foreign Office. The Beeb introduced the first teletext service, Ceefax, back in 1974. The BBC is one of the world's largest television production companies, as well as being the largest broadcast news gathering operation in the world.

Beefeaters

Beefeaters are the guards at the Tower of London, but they act more like tour guides these days. Their official title is 'Yeoman Warder of Her Majesty's Royal Palace and Fortress the Tower of London, and Members of the Sovereign's Body Guard of the Yeoman Guard Extraordinary.' Phew. King Henry VII formed the Body Guard in 1485 to uphold the dignity and grandeur of the English Crown for all time. The word 'yeoman' means 'man of the district', and Yeomen were in a class of their own, recognised by the state in the 14th and 15th centuries, wedged between the upper class and the labourers. They lived well and didn't have to starve in winter like their poorer neighbours. 'To make good infantry it requireth men bred not in a servile and indigent fashion, but in some free and plentiful manner' one statesman pronounced.

But why are they called Beefeaters? Well, Count Cosmo, the Grand Duke of Tuscany, noted on his travels in England in the 17th century that they were 'Eaters-of-Beef, of which a considerable portion is allowed them daily by the Court'. Even MPs at that time referred to them as such, the greedy so-and-sos.

In 2007, 42-year-old Moira Cameron became the first ever female Beefeater. If you would like to follow in her footsteps around the Tower, you must have retired from the armed forces after at least 22 years of service. You should also be prepared to take your work home with you – the yeomen and their families live in the Tower of London.

Boy Scouts

The Scouting Movement – or Woggle Wearers, as they are sometimes called – was founded by Robert Baden-Powell in 1908. His book *Scouting for Boys: A*

Handbook for Instruction in Good Citizenship was first published that year and was based on his boyhood experiences, his time with the Mafeking Cadet Corps during the Second Boer War and his experimental camp on Brownsea Island, Poole Harbour. Twenty boys from various backgrounds took part in the Brownsea Island experiment – the first Scout camp – over seven days in August 1907. Activities included camping, woodcraft and lifesaving. Baden-Powell's book went on to become one of the bestselling books of the 20th century and the movement rapidly grew to become the world's largest youth organisation. In 1910, a group of girls from Pinkneys Green in Berkshire approached Baden-Powell at a Boy Scout Rally at Crystal Palace and asked him to make them Scouts. A bit of 'rough and tumble' between boys and girls was just out of the question, so the Guide Movement was formed instead.

Changing of the Guard

The Queen's Guard is a company of soldiers from the same regiment, responsible for guarding Buckingham Palace and St James's Palace in London. Since the Queen's official residence is St James's, the Guard Commander is based there. The Queen's Guard is not just for show – sentries are on duty 24 hours a day, and also patrol the palace grounds. Guards used to be stationed outside the palace fences, but this practice ended in 1959 following an unfortunate incident involving a female tourist and a Coldstream Guardsman. Harassed by crowds of pesky tourists, the guard booted a female tourist during a march. Following a complaint against him, the poor fellow was confined to barracks for ten days, and from then on sentries remained within the confines of palace walls and fences.

The Guards change at 11am each day. The St James's Palace detachment march down the mall and join the Buckingham Palace detachment at Buckingham Palace. The 'Old Guard' then await the arrival of the 'New Guard', who have by then assembled at the Parade Barracks on Wellington Square. A 35-strong military band play while the Old Guard meet the New Guard, present arms and hand over the keys to the palace. The replacement sentries take their places at the two palaces, and the Old Guard march back to Wellington Square for a well-earned break.

The household have guarded the sovereign since 1660. Their famous bearskin hats are 18 inches tall and made from the fur of the Canadian black bear. Donned to create an illusion of height, the hats were worn during battle as late as the 19th century (by footguards during the Crimean War), although by then they were mostly limited to ceremonial wear, as they were rather expensive and impractical to boot.

Comic Relief

The British charity organisation that's given us Red Nose Day, as well as bringing joy into our living rooms every couple of years, was founded in 1985 by the comedy scriptwriter Richard Curtis to raise funds and awareness to try to alleviate famine in Africa. Inspiration for Comic Relief came from Amnesty International's comedy benefit show the *Secret Policeman's Ball*; and Jane Tewson, a notable charity worker, was the brains behind the concept. Noel Edmond launched Comic Relief on his *Late, Late Breakfast Show* on Christmas Day 1985 from a refugee camp in Sudan. The 'Golden Pound Principle' guarantees every last penny is spent on charitable projects. Everything else, such as staff salaries, is covered by corporate sponsors or interest earned on money raised. Comic Relief has raised a whopping £600 million for charity to date. And it's them we have to thank for the unforgettable charity single 'Living Doll', featuring the Young Ones and the legendary Cliff Richard.

Crown Jewels

Said to be worth £20 million, this glittering collection of finery has been housed in the Tower of London since 1303, guarded by Yeomen Warders – or Beefeaters. The jewels consist of all the regalia used by the sovereign during coronation – crowns, orbs, spurs and the like – as well as a unique collection of medals and royal christening fonts. Previously housed in the White Tower and Martin Tower, they now reside in the Jewel House, which receives millions of visitors every year.

Edward the Confessor put the first jewellery collection together in the 11th century, and the goodies were kept at Westminster Cathedral. However, a theft at the Abbey in 1303 was a cause for concern, and the precious collection was transferred to the Tower of London. There it remained for nearly 350 years until the downfall of the monarchy and the execution of Charles I in 1649, when Oliver Cromwell had most of the jewels melted down for coinage, showing his disdain for 'the detestable rule of kings'. Only three swords and a coronation spoon remained, but this was rectified with the restoration of the monarchy in 1660 – a new crown was made in time for Charles II's 1661 coronation. The same crown is used to this day, and is called St Edward's crown, because the gold is said to be from Edward the Confessor's crown. The orb and sceptre are the other essential ceremonial accessories, both of which were made in 1660. The orb consists of a golden ball attached to a jewel-covered cross, and only weighs three pounds. It symbolises the higher power of god above the monarch, while the sceptre – a golden stick covered with many a precious stone – is a symbol of the monarch's earthly powers.

Disguised as a priest, Colonel Thomas Blood ('Captain Blood') made off with a crown, a sceptre and an orb in 1671, but was caught at the East Gate of the Tower. However, the King was so impressed with Blood's ingenuity that he granted him a reprieve, and an annual pension to boot.

The jewels were temporarily removed from the Tower during the Second World War, though their whereabouts at that time is still a state secret.

MI5

Britain's security service, there to protect us from terrorists, spies and subversion, was founded in 1909. Britain and Germany were engaged in a naval arms race and there were numerous reports in the media of German spies and invasion plots. The

Weekly News even had its own 'Spy Editor', offering readers £10 a pop for information on German agents. The Committee of Imperial Defence, made up of the War Office and Admiralty, was established to review the situation, and it was agreed that a new Secret Service Bureau be established to coordinate efforts in intelligence. Captain Vernon GW Kell of the South Staffordshire Regiment and Captain Mansfield Cumming of the Royal Navy became the first heads of the new Bureau. It was subsequently divided into two sections: the Home Section, dealing with espionage within the UK, which became known as MI5 (Security Service), and the Foreign Section, gathering intelligence from abroad, MI6 (the Secret Intelligence Service). Although the Security Service only had 14 staff by 1914, they were still able to make considerable breakthroughs, and the Secret Intelligence Service managed to arrest more than 20 spies between 1909 and the outbreak of the First World War. Security headquarters are at 85 Vauxhall Cross, on the South Bank of the River Thames.

National Trust
Caring for more than 248,000 hectares of beautiful British countryside, as well as more than 700 miles of

coastline and 200 buildings and gardens, the National Trust is a national treasure in itself. It was founded by Miss Octavia Hill, Sir Robert Hunter and Canon Hardwicke Rawnsley in 1895 in response to burgeoning industrialisation and the lack of control over development. The trio set up the Trust to act as a guardian for the nation, aiming to acquire and protect threatened coastline, countryside and buildings. Octavia Hill famously said, 'The need of quiet, the need of air, the need of exercise, and the sight of sky and of things growing seem human needs, common to all men.' She had a point.

The trust's first property was Alfriston Clergy House, and its symbol – a sprig of oak leaves and acorns – is said to have been inspired by a carving in the house's cornices. The first nature reserve to be acquired was Wicken Fen, and White Barrow was the first archaeological monument.

These days the trust has over 3.5 million members, and relies on charitable donations for funding. The most bizarre donations came from a mysterious masked group who called themselves Ferguson's Gang – the group were made up entirely of women using silly pseudonyms and mock-Cockney accents to hide their identity, and their activities in the late 1920s raised enough money to fund the purchase of a mill and a town hall. Aside from its collection of houses, castles, nature reserves, pubs and inns, the trust looks after the national collection of lawnmowers along with 57 meat strainers, among other diverse and eccentric objects.

NHS

Britain's National Health Service was formally launched on 5 July 1948 by Health Secretary Aneurin Bevan. Before 1948, thousands died of infectious diseases in Britain every year and infant mortality was high (around 1 in 20 children died before their first birthday). Those who were too poor to pay for medical care upfront relied on home remedies, the charity of doctors willing to give of their time for free, and on voluntary hospitals. Workers were entitled to free access to a doctor, but that often didn't extend to their families. Philanthropists and social reformers could only do so much: it was too big a problem to be handled privately. The Dawson Report of 1920 recommended a comprehensive system, followed by the Royal Commission on National Health Insurance in 1926, which pioneered the idea of a publicly funded health service. The Second World War introduced the Emergency Medical Service, which was the first centrally funded service, and in 1942 Sir William Beveridge, an eminent economist, produced 'The Beveridge Report', which concluded that a national health service was an essential element of a viable social security system. Aneurin Bevan steered legislation through the Commons in November 1946. Everybody 'irrespective of means, age, sex or occupation' would have 'equal opportunity to benefit from the best and most up-to-date medical and allied services available'.

Oxbridge

Oxford and Cambridge are the two oldest universities in England, as well as being two of the most prestigious, with some of the world's most famous alumni. When English students were expelled from the University of Paris in 1167, Henry II, who had built Beaumont Palace near where Worcester College now stands, established Oxford as England's centre of learning. The first lecture in Oxford dates back to 1188, and was given by Gerald of Wales. From 1201 onwards, the head of the university became known as the Chancellor, and the *universitas* was recognised in 1231. Students from the north (including Scotland) and the south (including Ireland and Wales) were affiliated, and religious orders such as Dominicans and Franciscans provided housing from the 13th century onwards. Individual colleges, funded by private benefactors, were established around the same time, with Merton College becoming the model for Cambridge. Cambridge was founded in 1209 by scholars who had left Oxford after a dispute with local townsfolk. Both universities founded publishing houses – Oxford in 1478 and Cambridge in 1534. Rivalry between the two universities is alive and well, typified by the annual Oxford and Cambridge Boat Race. The first recorded instance of the word *Oxbridge* (a composite word referring to both Universities) is in William Thackeray's novel *Pendennis*, published in 1849.

Posh and Becks

With their spangly designer 'his and hers' outfits, and their far from posh accents, Posh and Becks are the Pearly King and Queen of British fashion. Victoria Adams was born in Essex on 17 April 1974, while David Beckham was born just over a year later, on 2 May 1975, in Leytonstone, East London. The young Victoria, who lived in posh Goffs Oak, Hertfordshire, used to be embarrassed when her dad dropped her off at school in his Rolls-Royce. Becks's mum was a hairdresser, his dad a kitchen fitter, and both were mad keen on Man United. Bullied and isolated at school, Posh found her true calling after watching the movie *Fame*, and went on to enrol at Laine Theatre Arts College, at around the same time Becks was completing a youth training scheme at Man United. Responding optimistically to an advertisement in *The Stage* in 1993 for someone 'able to sing and dance', Posh went on to join the Spice Girls. A year later, Becks was making his UEFA Champions League debut, scoring a goal in a 4–0 victory at home. By 1997, when they met at a charity football match, both were celebrities in their own right, and the golden couple were married two years later, seated on gold thrones in a castle in Ireland. It seems Posh had managed to get over her embarrassment about being rich. They went on to buy their multi-million-pound home, which has come to be known fondly as Beckingham Palace, and world domination quickly followed.

Public Schools

These days, public schools are secondary schools that charge fees and offer boarding facilities. But it wasn't always that way. Public schools have a long tradition, dating back to the formation of

Westminster School in 1179, when the Benedictine monks of Westminster Abbey were required by Pope Alexander III to provide a small charity school. In 1441, Henry VI founded Eton College to provide free education to 70 poor boys who would then go on to King's College, Cambridge. Life for the boys at Eton was pretty spartan. They slept two or three to a bed and were up at five every morning, chanting prayers while getting dressed. Public schools were open to public applicants at a time when other schools were privately owned and charged fees or children had personal tutors. Many of their applicants would have been young men from underprivileged backgrounds on scholarships. Public schools flourished from the mid-19th century, along with a curriculum based heavily on classics and physical activity for boys. But, by then, the poor, for whom these schools were originally established, were being overlooked in favour of the offspring of gentlemanly elite and the aspiring middle classes of Victorian Britain.

CHAPTER TWO

THE GOOD, THE BAD AND THE UGLY

'Will you quit your griping. I know there'll be
fireworks if we get caught...'

THE GOOD, THE BAD
AND THE UGLY

The Blitz

The British press gave the German word for 'lightning' to the heavy bombing raids carried out over Britain in 1940 and 1941 during the Second World War. It began on 7 September 1940. Casualties were high, and on the first day of bombing 430 people were killed and 1,600 badly injured, with the German Air Force dropping 5,300 tonnes of explosives on the capital in just over three weeks. Major coastal ports and centres of production were also vulnerable. Coventry had over 500 tonnes of explosives and nearly 900 incendiary bombs dropped on it in ten hours in November that same year. The British public had been warned: steel shelters were dug into gardens, larger shelters were built in towns and a blackout was strictly enforced, but that couldn't protect them. Raids were sometimes back-to-back, so people often stayed in their shelters rather than risk wandering home again. The government attempted to confuse the German bombers by ordering a blackout. Street lamps were left off, car headlights were covered and civilians hung black material in their windows at night. Venturing out at night was dangerous – cars often crashed and pedestrians walked into each other, fell off bridges or fell into ponds. After May 1941, the bombing raids eased when Hitler turned his focus to Russia. However, the Blitz was a devastating blow to the people of London: 60,000 people lost their lives, 87,000 were seriously injured and two million homes were destroyed.

Charles Darwin
Charles Darwin is the man we have to thank for laying down the foundations of the theory of evolution and consequently revolutionising the way we apprehend the natural world. Born on 12 February 1809 in Shrewsbury, Shropshire, he had a good start in life, with well-to-do parents and famous grandfathers on both sides – Josiah

Wedgwood, manufacturer of china, and Erasmus Darwin, a leading intellectual of the 18th century. As a child, Charles took a keen interest in nature, and went on to Edinburgh University to study medicine, where his friend John Edmonstone, a freed black slave, taught him taxidermy. He later switched to divinity at Cambridge where, rather than putting his head in his books, he pursued the craze for beetle collecting. In 1831, he joined a scientific expedition of the South American coastline on board the HMS *Beagle*, and it was during this trip that his ideas began to take shape. The rich variety of life he encountered, particularly in the Galapagos Islands, combined with his reading of Lyell's *Principles of Geology*, led him to the conclusion that species evolve by natural selection, which says that animals or plants most likely to survive are those that adapt to their environment and gradually change over time. He slogged away for 20 years before announcing the discovery, along with another naturalist, Alfred Russell Wallace, in 1858. The following year, his seminal work *On the Origin of Species by Means of Natural Selection* was published, although Darwin's theory that we were closely related to the apes found little favour with the Church. Darwin died on 19 April 1882 and was buried in Westminster Abbey. Some people still don't like his idea but, like it or lump it, it's a fact of science that we are 98 per cent chimpanzee. Genetically speaking, anyway.

Christopher Wren

The great architect Christopher Wren was born in Wiltshire in 1632. He was a sickly child, but went on to live a long and prosperous life, attending Oxford – where he studied Latin and the works of Aristotle – and later going on to become Professor of Astronomy at Gresham College. Wren played an active role in establishing England's major scientific body, the Royal Society, and his attention turned to architecture around the late 1660s, when he designed Pembroke College in Cambridge and the Sheldonian Theatre in Oxford. He was responsible for designing and rebuilding 51 churches after the Fire of London in 1665, including St Paul's Cathedral, before becoming the King's Surveyor of Works in 1669. He died at the age of 91.

David Attenborough

The man who brought us *Planet Earth* – no, not God, but David Attenborough – was born in London on 8 May 1926. David and his two brothers grew up on the campus of University College, Leicester, where his father was principal, and David spent his childhood collecting natural specimens before winning a scholarship to study geology and zoology at Clare College, Cambridge in 1945. He was called up for National Service in 1947 and spent two years stationed in North Wales and the Firth of Forth with the Royal Navy. A job application at the BBC was turned down in 1950, but he was invited back to complete a training course and began work as a producer for the Talks Department in 1952. After working behind the scenes at first (because his teeth were deemed too big for presenting), he eventually went on to present *The Pattern of Animals*, which featured residents of London Zoo. Attenborough was Controller at the BBC2 from 1965 to 1969, and he is the man to thank for bringing snooker to our screens and introducing colour television to Britain (very handy for the snooker fans). He was Director of Programmes from 1969 to 1972, but turned down an offer of promotion to Director General, preferring to resign his post and return to doing what he loved best, making documentaries. A good thing too, as he went on to produce and present some of the most spectacular wildlife programmes ever made – an estimated 500 million people worldwide watched the 13-part series *Life on Earth*, first transmitted in 1979.

Great Fire of London

The Great Fire of London was an accident waiting to happen. Most houses in 17th-century London were made of wood, and many had open fires. In 1666, a fire broke out in the King's bakery in Pudding Lane in the City and spread quickly, fanned by a stiff east wind. There was no fire brigade back in those days, so all the locals could do was attempt to douse the fire with buckets of water and beat the flames back with staves. It wasn't much use. Fearing sedition, King Charles handed over control to his brother, the duke of York, who set guards on to the streets to control the looting as people fled their houses. The price of a cart rose from £3 to £30 as Londoners poured out of the city. Samuel Pepys noted that many families chose to save their musical instruments, bizarrely. Valuables were hidden in sewers and refugee camps appeared on the high ground of Moorfields, Islington and Parliament Hill. The fire consumed the Guildhall and Old St Paul's Cathedral. 'The stones of Paul's flew like granados [grenades],' wrote the diarist John Evelyn.

The fire left 200,000 people destitute, and more than 13,000 houses, 87 churches and the main buildings in the City were all destroyed, though only five deaths were recorded. The cost of accommodation soared as modern London slowly rose from the ashes.

Great Plague

Aside from its sheer scale, there was nothing great about the Black Death or Bubonic Plague that arrived in Britain in 1665. It spread from the East, possibly China, and began in St Giles-in-the-Field in London, which was poor and overcrowded. Over the course of the summer, around 100,000 poor souls (a third of the population) died a horrible death. Skin turned black and was accompanied by inflamed glands in the groin, vomiting, a swollen tongue and a splitting headache. The disease took only four to six days to incubate and if it struck your home the house was sealed and the words 'Lord have mercy on us' daubed on your front door before you were left to perish. 'Bring out your dead' was the morbid call each evening, as bodies were carted off to huge pits that were soon overflowing. It was mostly the poor who suffered, of course, with the King and all his men, along with anyone else who could afford it, vacating the city. Good old Samuel Pepys stayed around to record everything, though. The nursery rhyme 'Ring-a-ring a roses' perfectly describes the symptoms of the plague – posies of flowers were believed to keep the plague away if held to the nose. London wasn't the only place that suffered. York was badly hit, and to this day no one has dared disturb the pits outside the city walls. Luckily enough the cold weather came, killing the fleas carrying the plague bacillus, while the Great Fire of London a year later did a good job of finishing off the remaining fleas and black rats.

Guy Fawkes
Guy Fawkes, who was born in York in 1570, liked to be called Guido, after a ten-year stint fighting for the Spanish Catholic cause. In 1605, English Catholics were being persecuted right, left and centre in James I's Britain. Thirteen young men, Fawkes among them, decided that the only thing to do was to blow up the Houses of Parliament and kill the King and the MPs who were making life so difficult, and the Gunpowder Plot was hatched. Fawkes's crew managed to get their hands on 36 barrels of gunpowder and stored them in a cellar just under the House of Lords. The plot was foiled when some of Guy's friends started to have doubts, fearing that innocents would be killed too. An anonymous letter was sent to Lord Monteagle warning, 'Retire yourself into the country for ... they shall receive a

terrible blow this Parliament and yet they shall not see who hurts them.' The letter made its way into the King's hands and the cellar was stormed on the morning of 5 November. Guido, who was hiding out there, was tortured and executed. That very night bonfires were set alight to celebrate the King's triumph, and thus the tradition of Bonfire Night began, with effigies of Guy Fawkes (and sometimes even the Pope) being burned across the land. To this day, the Queen won't enter Parliament until a thorough search of the cellars has been carried out by her Yeomen. And who can blame her.

Jack the Ripper

A whole industry has grown up around London's most infamous serial killer. At the time of these gruesome murders towards the end of the 19th century, the Great Famine in Ireland and the pogroms in Tsarist Russia and Eastern Europe had seen mass migration of Irish and Jewish refugees to England, which led to severe overcrowding and terrible conditions, particularly around the East End of London and the parish of Whitechapel. As many as 1,200 women 'of very low class', according to the police, were driven into prostitution. A great deal of police energy went into trying to contain the demonstrations by the hungry and dispossessed, and it was during this time that Jack the Ripper struck. The brutal attacks, which involved the mutilation and disembowelment of prostitutes, were widely reported in the media, and Scotland Yard received a series of letters from a writer claiming to be the perpetrator of these crimes. One letter, sent to the Whitechapel Vigilance Committee, was accompanied by a human kidney preserved in ethanol. The killer's name came about after a letter sent to the Central News Agency, promising to 'clip the ladys ear off' and signed 'Jack the Ripper' was published by the police. While Jack wasn't the first or worst killer the police had ever seen, he arrived at a time when the British media was burgeoning and so found worldwide notoriety. To this day, his identity remains a mystery, though over 100 suspects have been identified.

Margaret Thatcher

An icon to some, a pariah to others, Britain's first and only female prime minister was born Margaret Hilda Roberts, a grocer's daughter, on 13 October 1925 in Grantham, Lincolnshire. She studied at Oxford University and became a research chemist, before retraining to become a barrister in 1954. Margaret took Denis Thatcher's name when they were married in 1951, two years after meeting at a Paint Trades Federation function.

By the age of 34, Thatcher was Conservative MP for Finchley in North London. She served as a junior Minister for Pensions in Harold Macmillan's government and when Edward Heath became Prime Minister in 1970 Thatcher was appointed Secretary for Education, quickly earning herself the nickname 'Milk Snatcher' when free school milk for the over-sevens was abolished. She wasted no time in challenging Heath for (and winning) the leadership when the Conservatives were defeated in 1974, becoming Prime Minister five years later and winning three terms in office. Thatcher managed to reduce inflation but increase unemployment. She narrowly escaped with her life in 1984, when the IRA planted a bomb at a Conservative party conference in Brighton. She and US president, Ronald Reagan, were as thick as thieves, while the Soviets liked to refer to her as the 'Iron Lady'. Maggie's poll tax, which was based on the number of people living in a house rather than its estimated price and therefore targeted the poor, was hugely unpopular and she was ousted in 1990 in favour of the grey man of politics, John Major.

Queen Elizabeth II

Elizabeth Alexandra Mary was born in London on 21 April 1926 to Albert, Duke of York, and his wife, formerly Lady Elizabeth Bowes-Lyon, better known to us as the Queen Mum. Elizabeth Alexandra would have had little chance of becoming queen if it hadn't been for her uncle Edward's abdication (owing to his love of an American divorcee) when Liz was ten. Her father Albert then became George VI. The young princess was educated at home, and during the war evacuated to Windsor Castle with her sister Margaret in 1939. After training as a driver in the Women's Auxiliary Territorial Service in 1945, Elizabeth married her distant cousin Philip Mountbatten (formerly Prince Philip of Greece and Denmark) in 1947. Her father, the King, died on 6 February 1952 and she was crowned Queen at Westminster Abbey in June the following year, at the age of 27. The 1953 coronation was televised around the world, with an estimated 20 million people watching in Britain alone, along with 12 million more listening in on the radio.

She has reigned ever since, but not without incident. In what was dubbed 'the most gross and scandalous lapse of security in her 30-year reign', the Queen was abruptly awakened in her room by an intruder in 1982 and endured a bizarre ten minutes in the company of her visitor before help arrived. The 31-year-old Michael Fagan had evaded guardsmen, bobbies, servants, surveillance cameras and electronic devices to reach the royal bedroom, one flight up from the palace grounds, and the nation was gobsmacked. Luckily, Mr Fagan wasn't threatening, and only wanted to chat about the coincidence that both he and the monarch had four children. Despite a couple of calm calls to security, the Queen was only saved when a maid walked into the bedroom and exclaimed, 'Bloody hell, ma'am! What's he doing in there?'

Robin Hood

Robin Hood and dodgy market traders have a lot in common, stealing from the rich to give (or, in the case of the trader, sell at a knock-off price) to the poor. He also has quite a bit in common with modern-day terrorists, fond as he was of killing landowners and waging guerrilla war against the authorities. It's generally believed that Robin Hood, if he really existed, lived sometime in the 13th century. William Langland refers to him in his poem of 1377, 'The vision of William concerning Piers Plowman': 'I do not know my paternoster perfectly as the priest sings it. / But I know the rhymes of Robin Hood and Randolph, earl of Chester.' Others think he may have been around earlier, perhaps even as far back as the 11th century. We usually think of Robin as hailing from Sherwood Forest, but evidence from early ballads would suggest that he was a yeoman from the Barnsdale area of South Yorkshire. There are at least eight references to one 'Rabunhod' in regions across England between 1261 and 1300, but it could simply be shorthand for any fugitive or outlaw. The name is again used in 1439 to describe an itinerant felon in a petition presented to Parliament. And Guy Fawkes and his associates were branded 'Robin Hoods' in 1605.

Tony Blair

Tony Blair stepped down as Prime Minister in June 2007, after winning three elections and waging five wars. Born in Edinburgh in 1953, the first few years of his life were spent in Adelaide, Australia, where his father was lecturing in law. Upon their return to the UK, the Blairs moved to Durham, and the young Tony boarded at Fettes in Edinburgh. He was, according to one housemaster, 'full of himself and very argumentative'. He was even threatened with expulsion, but his girlfriend's father came to his rescue. Tony spent a year managing rock bands and stacking shelves in London before heading off to Oxford to study law and front a rock band called Ugly Rumours. Blair joined the Labour Party shortly before leaving university with a second-class degree to become a trainee barrister. He met Cherie Booth, a fellow trainee, and the couple married in 1980 and set up home in Hackney. Their neighbour, Charles Clarke, encouraged their interest in politics.

Blair secured a seat in Sedgefield – near where he grew up – in the 1983 elections. He didn't hide the fact that he thought the Labour Party had to appeal to the middle classes or die, and he was denounced by some as a 'traitor to socialism'. When the Labour leader John Smith died suddenly in 1994, Tony Blair was drafted in. Blair, considered a bit of a lightweight, was dubbed 'Bambi' by the British press, so he hired former tabloid journalist Alastair Campbell to sharpen up his image. He aligned himself with 'cool Britannia', tapping into the optimistic mood of the Nineties, and swept to a landslide victory in 1997, becoming the youngest Prime Minister in nearly 200 years.

Winston Churchill

The British Bulldog of politics had a noble beginning at Blenheim Palace in Oxfordshire in

1874. He attended Sandhurst before embarking on an army career, and was made a prisoner-of-war while working as a journalist during the Boer War, but luckily escaped. At the tender age of 26, he became a Conservative MP, before crossing over to join the Liberal Party four years later. It was a fortuitous move: the Liberals won the 1905 election and 'Winnie' was appointed undersecretary at the Colonial Office. By 1910, he was Home Secretary, and was made First Lord of the Admiralty the following year, although he had to resign after a disastrous campaign in Gallipoli.

After serving for a time on the Western Front, he was back in government by 1917 as Minister of Munitions, then went on to become Secretary of State for War and Air and Chancellor of the Exchequer.

Churchill's support for Edward VIII over his relationship with the divorcee Wallis Simpson, his opposition to Indian self-rule and his warnings about the encroaching Nazi invasion all made him unpopular over the next few years. When war broke out, however, Churchill was the man everyone turned to: he took Neville Chamberlain's place when he resigned as Prime Minister in 1940. He stood down in the 1945 election, but was PM again between 1951 and 1955.

As well as being PM twice, he managed to win himself a Nobel Prize for Literature. Churchill's history of the First World War appeared in four volumes under the title of *The World Crisis* (1923–29); his memoirs of the Second World War ran to six volumes (1948–1953/54). After his retirement from office, Churchill wrote the four-volume *History of the English-speaking Peoples* (1956–58). His wonderful oratory lives on in a dozen volumes of speeches, among them *The Unrelenting Struggle* (1942), *The Dawn of Liberation* (1945) and *Victory* (1946).

Churchill was rarely seen without a cigar in his hand, and they had to be Cuban. The great man adored them, and was always at pains to ensure abstinence would not be forced upon him. The story goes that, when about to take his first high-altitude plane flight in an unpressurised cabin during the war, the Prime Minister was provided with a custom-made oxygen mask that would accommodate his habit while airborne. The mask contained a special hole which allowed him to puff away happily at 15,000 feet.

CHAPTER THREE
FAMOUS LANDMARKS

'The speaker fell on him.'

FAMOUS LANDMARKS

Angel of the North

Standing on a hill at the head of the Team Valley in Gateshead, this 66ft steel Angel is one of the UK's most recognisable landmarks. Work began on this monumental sculpture in 1994 – the same year its creator, Antony Gormley, won the prestigious Turner Prize – and was completed in 1998. It used 600 metric tonnes of concrete for the foundations, to anchor the sculpture to the rock below, as it has to endure winds of over 100mph. It was created in three parts, at Hartlepool Steel Fabrications Ltd, using Corten weather-resistant steel. The form, which is based on the artist's body, is over five storeys high (just over 20 metres), and its wingspan is wider than the Statue of Liberty is long (54 metres). The body is hollow, with a handy access door high up on a shoulder blade. It's viewed by at least 90,000 motorists a day and is built to last more than a hundred years. 'The angel has three functions,' according to Gormley, 'firstly a historic one to remind us that below this site coal miners worked in the dark for two hundred years; secondly to grasp hold of the future expressing our transition from the industrial to the information age, and lastly to be a focus for our hopes and fears.' Locals fondly refer to it as 'The Gateshead Flasher'.

Big Ben

There's no mistaking this most famous of British tourist attractions, although Big Ben is the name of the great bell inside, rather than the tower itself. The crowning glory of the Houses of Parliament, the impressive clock tower looms 315 feet above the River Thames. It was designed by Augustus Pugin (the architect's final design before he lost his marbles and died) and erected in 1859. Pisa isn't the only place with a leaning tower. Big Ben leans ever so slightly to the northwest, thanks to the tunnelling for London Underground's Jubilee Line.

As for Big Ben himself, the great bell was cast in

1856 by Warners of Norton near Stockton-on-Tees and transplanted by sea to London. On arrival at the Port of London, it was placed on a carriage and pulled across Westminster Bridge by 16 white horses. First hung in New Palace Yard, it was tested every day until 17 October 1857, when a one-metre crack appeared. Nobody would accept the blame, and Warners quoted too high a price to recast the bell, so George Mears at the Whitechapel Foundry was called in. George cast the second bell in April 1858. It was too large to fit up the clock tower's shaft vertically so Big Ben was turned on its side and winched up. It took 30 hours to get the bell into the belfry in October 1858. So far, so good. Big Ben rang out the following year but its success was short-lived. In September 1859, it cracked again and remained silent for four years while the hour was struck on the fourth quarter bell. A solution to Big Ben's silence was eventually found in 1863, when Sir George Airy, the Astronomer Royal, suggested the bell should be turned a quarter (so the hammer struck a different spot), a lighter hammer used and a small square cut into the Bell to prevent the crack from worsening. It worked, and has kept perfect time ever since, even managing to chime throughout the Blitz. The tower is open to the general public, but a visit must be arranged through your local MP. But be warned, there are no elevators and guests must climb 334 steps to reach the top. The clock's timekeepers have a stack of pre-decimal pennies which they add or remove to the pendulum to minutely alter the time – adding one penny causes the clock to gain two-fifths of a second in 24 hours.

Big Ben may have been named after Sir Benjamin Hall, who oversaw the installation of the great bell, or after English Heavyweight Boxing Champion Benjamin Caunt.

The 'bongs' of Big Ben can be heard on ITN's News at Ten, on BBC Radio 4 and on the BBC World Service. Its chimes are also broadcast to mark the 11th hour of the 11th day of the 11th month on Remembrance Day. And of course it's Big Ben that rings in the New Year.

Blackpool Tower
Blackpool Tower, Britain's emblem of seaside fun, was conceived of by hotelier and town councillor John Bickerstaff, who fell in love with the newly built Eiffel Tower, or 'truly tragic street lamp', while visiting Paris and decided it was just what Blackpool needed. Wasting no time in setting up the Blackpool Tower Company in 1891, height-obsessed John

somehow managed to convince the cotton barons of Burnley, Blackburn and Preston to donate the £290,000 (that's £40 million in today's money) needed to build the Tower. It took three years to construct and used 2,500 tons of steel. Both of its architects, Maxwell and Tuke, died before its completion in 1894 – just four years after the Eiffel Tower was erected.

The Tower is 518 feet tall, and constructed in such a way that if it were to collapse it would fall into the Irish Sea.

When it opened to the public, thrillseekers paid sixpence to get in and another sixpence to take a lift to the top. The Tower remained in recreational use until the Second World War, when it was used as an RAF radar station, imaginatively known as 'RAF Tower'. It hasn't been modified much since, although the top was painted silver in 1977 to mark the Queen's Silver Jubilee, and in 1984 a giant model of King Kong was attached to its side. They say Bickerstaff, who later went on to be Lord Mayor of Blackpool, loved the Tower so much he couldn't bear to leave it. Perhaps this explains the sightings over the years of an elderly gentleman in Victorian period dress…

Buckingham Palace

Buckingham Palace has served as the official London residence of Britain's sovereigns since 1837 and today is the administrative headquarters of the monarch. First called Buckingham House, it was originally the Duke of Buckingham's (rather large) townhouse, built in 1703, and bought by George III in 1761 for his wife Queen Charlotte in 1761. Conveniently close to St James's Palace, it became known as the Queen's House. Their son, George IV, decided to turn the house into a palace and instructed the architect, John Nash, to double its size. But the King never moved in. However, the palace almost became the government's new home in 1834, following a fire at the Houses of Parliament, but in the end it went to Queen Victoria, who moved in in 1837, just three weeks after her accession to the throne. Buckingham Palace has remained a royal residence ever since.

With 775 rooms – including 19 state rooms, 52 royal and guest bedrooms, 188 staff bedrooms, 92 offices and 78 bathrooms – there's plenty of space for the 50,000 people who visit the palace each year as guests to banquets, lunches, dinners, receptions and the royal garden parties.

Hadrian's Wall

Hadrian's Wall, stretching 73 miles across the island from Wallsend-on-Tyne to Bowness on the Solway Firth, was constructed by the Emperor Hadrian in 122 AD in an effort to protect the northern reaches of the Roman Empire from prickly Pictish tribes of Scotland. The wall took eight years to complete with the help of legionaries from as far afield as Africa and Asia. Stone and turf were used to build the wall, and a road – known as the Stangate – ran alongside it to provide access. Milecastles (fortified structures spaced out every – you guessed it – mile along the wall) housed garrisons of up to 60 men, with watchtowers every third mile offering extra protection. After the Romans left – around 410 AD – locals helped themselves to the stone to build houses, while road building in the 18th century also made a few dents in the wall. But despite all this it's still standing, and is protected by UNESCO as a world heritage site.

Hyde Park

London's Hyde Park used to be part of the Manor of Eia, owned by the monks of Westminster Abbey. Westbourne Stream ran through it from Hampstead to the Thames. In 1536, the monasteries were dissolved and Henry VIII seized the land for himself, greedily creating his own private deer-hunting park. Charles I was a touch more magnanimous, and opened it to the general public in 1637. Its green spaces quickly became a popular destination, particularly on May Day. A few years later, the Great Plague saw Londoners flocking to the park in the hope of escaping the disease. William III moved to Kensington Palace towards the end of the 17th century and had 300 oil lamps installed along Rotten Row – or Route de Roi (King's Road) – as it would have been known then, making it the first road in England to be lit at night. The Serpentine – a 28-acre recreational lake –was constructed in 1728 under Queen Caroline – herself a keen gardener – by damming Westbourne Stream. In 1851, the Crystal Palace was erected for the Great Exhibition, and later moved to Sydenham in South London.

London Eye
Although not the first of its kind in London ('The Great Wheel of London' – which could hold 1,600 people – was erected in Earl's Court in 1895 and closed in 1906), the London Eye is the biggest ferris wheel in Europe and the UK's number-one paid tourist destination. With over 30 million visitors to

date, it has become a true icon of Britain. Perched like a giant bicycle wheel on the edge of the Thames, at the western end of the Jubilee Gardens on the South Bank, the Eye was formally opened by Prime Minister Tony Blair on 31 December 1999, but technical difficulties meant its doors remained closed to the public until March 2000. The structure holds 32 egg-shaped pods, each representing a different borough of London and able to hold 25 people. One revolution takes 30 minutes, and the wheel moves so slowly that people can walk on and off without it having to stop (though it can stop to allow the elderly and disabled to embark and disembark safely). Originally known as the Millennium Wheel, it was only supposed to remain on the South Bank for five years, but, thanks to its popularity and fantastic views, Lambeth Council agreed to make London's beloved wheel a permanent fixture.

Speakers' Corner

Occupying the northeast corner of Hyde Park, this bastion of liberty is on the site of Tyburn, one of London's 'hanging fields' and the place where Oliver Cromwell's two-year-old corpse was dragged and hung from the gallows in January 1661 as a warning to other would-be dissenters. They were hanged by the neck from morning. Cromwell in a green seare cloth, very fresh embalmed; Ireton (his son-in-law) … hung like a dried rat,' one eyewitness reported.

Riots broke out in Hyde Park in 1855 over the Sunday Trading Bill (which forbade trade on the Sabbath even though it was the only day your average working man had free). If you believe Karl Marx, this was the beginning of the English revolution and, according to Leslie James, Speakers' Corner was a fitting location for 'the century of the common man' to commence. The Chartist Movement used Hyde Park to hold protest demonstrations, as did the Reform League. Finally, the Parks Regulation Act was introduced in 1872, delegating responsibility to the park authorities rather than central government to permit meetings. Since then, it has become a traditional place for public speeches of any kind, with many a polemicist to be seen, especially on the weekends. Hecklers are welcomed too. Some of Speakers' Corner's most famous orators have included Karl Marx, Vladimir Lenin and George Orwell.

Tower of London
Part palace, part fortress, and part prison, the Tower of London sits next to Tower Bridge in East London.

William the Conqueror built the tower between the Thames and the ancient Roman city walls shortly after his coronation in 1066. The White Tower, housing the Chapel of St John, loomed large over the humble wooden buildings of medieval London, symbolising the Normans' stranglehold on the city. There were so many home improvements and extensions over the years that it is a veritable smorgasbord of architectural style – the formidable fortress we see today was complete by 1350.

As well as a royal residence, it was, of course, a prison, and traditionally the monarch spent the night prior to his or her coronation in the Tower, which must have been slightly unnerving considering how many monarchs lost their life here. A popular form of execution at the Tower was hanging, drawing and quartering – Guy Fawkes and William Wallace were among the poor unfortunates to meet their end this way.

Between 1914 and 1916, several spies were held and subsequently executed there, including Franz Buschmann. The last execution there, of the German Josef Jakobs, took place in 1941, the same year that Hitler's Deputy Führer Rudolf Hess was one of the last state prisoners at the Tower.

The site is also famous for its resident ravens,

tended to by the Raven Master. Legend has it that if they leave the Tower will collapse, along with the entire kingdom. The Crown Jewels were moved there in 1303, along with the Beefeaters, who guard the tower night and day, and help tourists navigate the site. Tourists were first allowed in during the 19th century, and, by the end of Queen Victoria's reign in 1901, over half a million people were crossing the moat every year.

White Cliffs of Dover

One of the UK's great natural wonders, the chalk cliffs of Dover were formed over 80 million years. But it took Vera Lynn, the singer from East Ham, to bring them worldwide recognition. With her song 'There'll be bluebirds over the White Cliffs of Dover ...', written by Walter Kent and Nat Burton, and released in 1942, the cliffs came to symbolise hope for peace in a time of bitter world conflict.

CHAPTER FOUR

TRANSPORT
AND TRAVEL

TRANSPORT AND TRAVEL

A–Z

London would be a mystery to us all were it not for this pocket-sized map of the capital. The *A–Z* was designed by a portrait painter by the name of Phyllis Pearsall. After getting lost on her way to a party in Belgravia one night in 1935, with the 1919 Ordnance Survey Map to hand, she came up with the idea of mapping London herself. She set off from her bedsit on Horseferry Road each morning at 5am, walking (and cataloguing) the 23,000 streets of the city, and clocking up 3,000 miles along the way. She kept her jottings in a shoebox under her bed. The good woman's working day was 18 hours long and she drew up the map with the help of a single draughtsman,

James Duncan. Unable to find a publisher, Phyllis founded the Geographer's Map Company in 1936, and printed 10,000 copies herself. She delivered 250 copies to W.H. Smith in a wheelbarrow, and more orders came flooding in soon after. The war years were tough for business as there were official restrictions on map production, despite the influx of foreign troops to the city, but after the war Phyllis overcame the paper shortages by having her atlases printed in the Netherlands. Other editions for Manchester, Liverpool, Birmingham, Edinburgh, Canterbury, Bath and Oxford followed, though the London map remains the most recognisable. All the *A–Z* maps print a non-existent trap street so that they can tell if a map has been illegally copied from theirs. Where a new, as yet unnamed street is being constructed, the *A–Z* map will include a made-up name. One such trap street was Bartlett Place, which was subsequently given its official name, Broadway Walk. Phyllis carried on painting and publishing until her death in 1996, a month before her 90th birthday.

Black Cab

The distinctive modern black cab – or hackney cab – the pride of the nation's capital, dates back to 1948, although its origins go back as far as 1662, when the first hackney-carriage licences were approved. These were for horse-drawn carriages, later hansom cabs, that operated as vehicles for hire. Electric hackney carriages appeared on the scene in 1901, and then gradually cars began to replace horse-drawn models, until the last horse-drawn hackney carriage went out of operation in 1947. The black cab – of which there are 21,000 in London – is allowed to look for passengers, whereas private-hire vehicles, or minicabs, can only pick up passengers who have previously booked. Many black cabs have a turning circle of only 25ft, one reason being that London's famous Savoy Hotel's entrance roundabout is so small. Such is the appeal of the black cab that celebrities such as Stephen Fry and Prince Philip choose to drive their own.

Cabbies have to pass a test called The Knowledge, an intensive training course, initiated in 1865, which requires an in-depth knowledge of London's streets and takes up to four years to complete. It's usually passed on the twelfth attempt. *The Blue Book* contains the 320 standard routes or 'runs' the would-be-cabbies – or 'Knowledge Boys' – have to memorise as they scoot around London with clipboards fixed to the handlebars of their bikes. Some 25,000 streets are covered within a six-mile radius of Charing Cross, along with general points of interest such as hotels, theatres and tube stations. Research by the Wellcome Department of Imaging Neuroscience confirms that doing The Knowledge actually makes your brain bigger, which probably explains why cabbies always seem to know about everything from football fixtures to politics.

British Rail

There's only one thing more boring than waiting for a train and paying silly money for the privilege of doing so, and that's reading about the origins of British Rail, so, forget it, I won't go there.

Little Chef

The first Little Chef – the roadside restaurant that makes those long journeys a little more bearable – opened its doors to the public in Reading in 1958, the year of Britain's first motorway. It had just 11 seats and was modelled after an American roadside diner. By the 1980s, Little Chef was a well-known fixture along our highways and byways, catering for weary salespeople and grumpy families alike. The Little Chef Lodge was established (later to be rebranded the Travelodge) and Little Chefs popped up in motorway service areas, later known as

'Welcome Breaks', throughout the land. In 2004, an attempt was made to produce a more svelte, healthier-looking chef on the logo but the project was abandoned. In its heyday, there were 400 Little Chef restaurants, but now there are only 180, although they still welcome over 20 million customers a year and feed them 10 million cups of tea, 12 million rashers of bacon, 10 million eggs and 13 million sausages. Rather a lot for a chef so little.

Lollipop Lady

A trip to school wouldn't be the same without the Lollipop Lady. The School Crossing Patrol was officially introduced by the Metropolitan Service as part of The London Traffic Law of 1953. This allowed any person authorised by the Commissioner of the Police to stop traffic, using the prescribed traffic sign, to let children cross. Drivers who didn't stop were fined. These days, the local authorities are responsible for providing school crossings and lollipop ladies (and gentlemen), although it's not a legal requirement, and they're rapidly becoming one of Britain's endangered species.

London Underground

This world famous underground – or 'tube', as it's

better known (owing to the shape of the tunnels) – serves a large swathe of Greater London as well as parts of Essex, Hertfordshire and Buckinghamshire. The world's first underground railway – the Metropolitan Railway linking Paddington Station and Farringdon Street via King's Cross – was opened on 10 January 1863. Within months, it was carrying over 26,000 passengers a day. By the end of the 19th century, the Metropolitan had extended its lines to Buckinghamshire, creating new suburbs along the way in what came to be known as Metro-land, now our commuter belt. The various railway operators agreed to try to jointly promote 'the Underground' in 1908, but it wasn't until 1933 that they became part of an integrated transport system under London Transport. A free map, designed by Harry Beck, was issued and immediately became a design classic, an updated version of which is still in use today.

Underground stations were used as shelters throughout the Blitz – they even provided bunks, latrines and catering facilities. Several stations were converted into government offices: for instance, Down Street (no longer in use) was used by the War Cabinet before the Cabinet War Rooms were completed. It's only since 1985, when the government created London Underground Limited

(LUL), that the underground has become a single entity. LUL is now owned by Transport for London (TfL), which is run by a board and a commissioner appointed by the Mayor of London. There are 270 stations on the London Underground and about 400 kilometres of track, making it the longest metro system in the world.

Mini

The 20th century's second most influential car and Britain's most popular car *ever*, the Mini began life in 1957. Leonard Lord, then head of the British Motor Corporation, was fed up with the sight of so many cheap German cars on the roads. 'God damn these bloody awful bubble cars,' he said. 'We must drive them off the road by designing a proper miniature car.' And so they did: a car less than ten feet long was designed by a team led by Sir Alex Issigonis, and was named the Mini, for obvious reasons. It hit the road in 1959, and was popularised by the likes of The Beatles (who drove a psychedelic model in *The Magical Mystery Tour*) and the then doyenne of British cool, Princess Margaret. Cheap as chips and hip to boot, it even managed to steal the limelight from Michael Caine in the famous 1969 heist film *The Italian Job*. And if that's not enough street cred for one car, the police in Barbados were using the Mini Moke up until recently. The souped-up Mini Cooper was introduced in 1961, and, alas, the last proper Mini (a red Cooper Sport) was built on 4 October 2000.

Rolls-Royce

The Rolls-Royce is synonymous with old-fashioned British charm and sophistication – not to mention luxury only affordable to the very wealthy. Henry Royce started an electrical and mechanical business in 1884, and made his first car in Manchester in 1904. That same year, he met Charles Rolls, proprietor of a motor-car dealership in Fulham. Rolls was impressed with Royce, and vice versa, so Rolls agreed to sell Royce's cars, the first of which was unveiled at the Paris Salon in December 1904. Production began in 1908.

The lineage of Rolls-Royce models is an impressive one. There's the Grey Ghost from 1905, and the Silver Ghost, made from 1906 to 1925 (considered by many to be the finest Roller ever made), which could achieve 0 to 60 mph in an incredible 18 seconds. Silver Ghosts were so tough and durable that the chassis was chosen as the undercarriage for the 8,000lb armoured cars the British used in the First World War. Then there's the

Phantom I of 1926; the 160-hp Phantom II of 1929; the 1936 Phantom III; and so on, through the Silver Wraiths, Silver Dawns, Silver Clouds and Silver Shadows that followed.

Despite the company's early successes and increasing reputation for faultless workmanship and stunning engineering, Charles Rolls's craving for speed and excitement got the better of him. After being taken for an aeroplane ride by Wilbur Wright, Rolls began losing interest in cars. He bought his own Wright-designed plane and was killed in a crash in 1910 when the plane's tail fell off during a flying display. He was the first Briton to be killed in an aeronautical accident, and the 11th internationally.

Royce was left to manage the company alone, but he eventually had a breakdown due to overwork. After recovering his health, he never again ventured into the factory, but chose to run the company by mail from his south of France villa. Royce's letters to his managers were packed with engineering and design specifications, and company executives bound the information into a volume referred to as 'The Bible'. Though Royce died in 1933, The Bible's closely guarded secret is still used for reference today, and company decisions are often made according to whether 'Henry Royce would have done it'.

After Royce's death, the silver nameplate on the distinctive Rolls-Royce grille – which had always been engraved 'RR' in red – was engraved in black.

Today Rolls-Royces are as close to handmade as one could hope for. The production line makes only 20 a week, and the finished cars are tested and retested, then tested again before they are sold. It has been said that, after they are sold, Rolls-Royce sees to it that they are serviced as if each owner were a member of the royal family.

Routemaster Bus

The hop-on-hop-off bus, with its red exterior and open platform at the rear, was one of London's most recognisable features. A bus conductor collected fares while the bus was moving, which made it ideal for London's busy streets. The Routemaster was introduced by London Transport in 1956 and was advanced for its time, possessing independent front suspension, power steering, fully automatic gearbox and power-hydraulic braking. The first bus in London, back in 1829, was a horse-drawn carriage from Paddington to Bank. It was named an 'omnibus' – meaning 'for all' – although most Londoners couldn't afford the one shilling fare. In 1898, the first motor bus appeared in London. Buses, trams and trains all vied for right of way on the capital's busy streets in the early 20th century, with buses proving more popular than trams, which went out of business in 1952. Trolleybuses (a cross between a tram and a bus) were widespread just before the Routemaster arrived, but the cost of maintaining the overhead wires and the decrease in the price of petrol (which helped the plight of motor buses) meant they soon became defunct. Our favourite red double-deckers had been phased out of public use by the end of 2005 in favour of more economic and reliable designs. It was argued that the increasingly old Routemasters were not wheelchair or buggy friendly, and that they were dangerous: an average of three people a year were killed getting on or off them. Nonetheless, they are much missed on London's streets, and luckily two 'heritage routes' remain: routes 9 and 15. More good news is that you can pick up a retired bus for around £2,000, and all you need is a standard driving licence to take up to eight passengers.

Sleeping Policemen

Why on earth should a speed bump be called a sleeping policeman? Simple, they are there to take the place of the beloved bobby on the beat and reduce traffic in residential areas to a crawl.

Figuratively speaking, the dozy coppers are *sleeping*, prostrate on the road. Manmade road bumps weren't necessary until the 20th century, as vehicles simply couldn't travel fast enough to warrant them until the advent of the automobile and the widespread use of smooth roads.

The origins of the bump are a little obscure, but it is thought the world's first bump was built in Chatham, New Jersey. In 1906, a *New York Times* article reported plans for Chatham crosswalks to be raised five or six inches above the road level, stating, 'This scheme of stopping automobile speeding has been discussed by different municipalities, but Chatham is the first place to put it into practice.'

Another story relating to the evolution of the sleeping policeman goes back to the Second World War. US Army Colonel Edgar Rothkrug, an engineer for the Army Corps of Engineers in New Guinea, was testing amphibious tanks (viable on land and water), and was irritated by the dangerous speeds at which the Military Police were driving tanks and cars across the yard between the warehouse to the boat launch ramp. Rothkrug ordered his men to pour down some concrete to create a raised bump to slow vehicles down. It worked a treat, especially because cars didn't have seatbelts – if soldiers did not slow down they were ejected from their jeeps. Apparently, the army patented the speed bump, and called it the 'Rothkrug bump', but this may just be a diverting story.

Either way, these irritating, but effective, obstacles come in all shapes and sizes these days: there's the road hump, the speed table, the speed cushion and the rumble strip, to name but a few. Local residents throughout the UK have campaigned to have sleeping policemen removed, citing noise pollution, damage to vehicles and the impeding of emergency services. That's what you get for sleeping on the job.

Traffic Wardens

Poor old traffic wardens, they do have a hard time of it – although perhaps unsurprisingly, considering they're paid to make our lives miserable. The first UK parking meters were installed outside the American Embassy in London, and two years later in 1961, following the Road Traffic Act of 1960, traffic wardens made their first appearance on the streets of the capital. They began with a 'testing day for tact and tempers', but it seems they didn't know what they were letting themselves in for, although abuse, and even violence, from drivers has always gone with the job.

In fact, violent attacks on road authorities date back centuries. The trouble all started when Parliament created the first 'turnpike trust' in 1706, allowing local commissions to demand fees from road users. The first turnpike gates were 'burnt, pull'd down and destroy'd' by coal merchants two days after being erected in Bristol in 1727. A few years later, a riot broke out when hundreds of farmers attempted to storm a jail and free three men accused of burning down a toll booth. Two culprits were hanged. Ingenious farmers in Wales dressed up as women to destroy toll booths and attack wardens, calling themselves 'Daughters of Rebecca', after the Biblical character who was told 'let thy seed possess the gates of those which hate them'.

Little seems to have changed over the years. In 1963, angry farmer Peter Hicks rigged his Land Rover with an electrical device to ward off traffic wardens – as touching the car produced a nasty electric shock. Hicks was apprehended by police but evaded prosecution. In June 2000, 31 police forces issued body armour to traffic wardens after a spate of attacks from angry drivers, and these days people resort to blowing up parking meters and assaulting traffic wardens an average of three times a day.

CHAPTER FIVE
LAW AND ORDER

'Could you just sign it *Bobby*?'

LAW AND ORDER

Bobbies

The British policeman is recognised worldwide, mainly thanks to his portrayal in countless TV dramas. Peelers, or 'Bobbies', as they're more commonly known, were named after their founder Home Secretary, and later Prime Minister, Sir Robert Peel – Bob being short for Robert. Following the success of the Royal Irish Constabulary, which Peel founded in 1812, the Metropolitan Police Act was passed in 1829, providing permanently appointed and salaried constables in the UK. The uniform of blue tailcoats and top hats was carefully chosen to help the Bobbies blend in with the sombre attire of that day. Officers were issued with a wooden truncheon (carried in the tail of their coats), a pair of handcuffs and a wooden rattle (not for playing with but for raising the alarm), although the rattle was replaced by a whistle (way more fun) in the 1880s. You had to be at least 6ft tall to be a policeman. Working seven days a week, with only five days' unpaid annual holiday and a salary of one bob a week, there were no laughing policemen back then. They weren't allowed to vote and had to ask permission to get married or even to share a meal with a friend, which can't have been much fun, as they had to wear their uniforms off duty. Funnily enough, the only major town which elected not to have its own separate police force was Bury, Peel's birthplace.

Robert Peel was thrown from his horse while riding on Constitution Hill in London on 29 June 1850, and died three days later.

Houses of Parliament

One of the world's most iconic buildings, the Palace of Westminster, as it is also known, is home to the House of Lords and the House of Commons. In medieval times, the site was known as Thorney Island. A royal palace was built here around the same time as Westminster Abbey in 1045. Westminster Hall, the oldest existing part of the palace, dates back to the end of the 11th century, while the Jewel Tower was built around 1365. The first official Parliament of England met here in 1295. After a fire gutted the building in 1529, Henry VII moved to St James's Palace, leaving the building to the politicians. The House of Lords originally met in the Queen's Chamber, while the House of Commons held its debates in Westminster Abbey, and then moved to St Stephen's Chapel. Christopher Wren was commissioned to carry out major work on the chapel in the late 17th century, and the palace was substantially remodelled by Sir John Soane in the early 19th century. The Medieval House of Lords chamber, which had been the target of the famed Gunpowder Plot of 1605, was demolished as part of this work. A fire broke out on 16 October 1834, destroying most of the palace. Buckingham Palace was considered as an alternative parliamentary residence but a new Gothic-style palace, designed by Charles Barry, was built instead. Begun in 1840, it took 30 years to complete. During the Blitz, the Houses of Parliament were hit 14 times and the Commons Chamber subsequently had to be rebuilt.

As you might expect, members of the House of Parliament are subject to all manner of rules and regulations. Smoking has been banned since the 17th century and eating in the chamber is not allowed, although the chancellor is permitted an alcoholic drink while delivering the Budget. Hats are beyond the pale, as are military medals and decorations. Hands must be kept out of pockets at all times, and swords must be left at home. MPs must not use names – 'my honourable friend' for same party members or 'the honourable lady/gentleman' for individuals from other parties must suffice. Newspapers may not be read in the chamber, and speeches cannot be read out – only notes may be used. Applause is disapproved of, and the name of the monarch cannot be referred to unless the Speaker has granted permission.

Magna Carta

The bedrock of English justice and freedom was issued by King John in 1215. John had been excommunicated in a quarrel over the appointment of the Archbishop of Canterbury and used money extracted from the Church to create a fledgling English Navy and invade Ireland in 1210, and then France in 1214, but he was forced to retreat back to England. Some rebel barons had had enough of his cowardly behaviour and appointed Robert FitzWalter as their leader. FitzWalter was a bit of a gangster – when his son-in-law was being tried for murder, he once turned up at court with 500 armed knights. London opened its gates to the rebels on 17 May 1215 and John was forced to engage in tricky negotiations which eventually led to the signing of Magna Carta. With Magna Carta, King John placed himself and England's future sovereigns and magistrates within the rule of law.

News at Ten

Britain's flagship news programme began life as *Late Night News* on ITV back in 1955. It was just 14 minutes long, and was broadcast at random times in the evening. It was only in 1967, after ten years of persuasion on the part of then editor Geoffrey Cox, that the Independent Television Authority (ITN) was pinned down to a 13-week trial run of a 30-minute show. Over the years, presenters have included Selina Scott and Anna Ford. ITV took issue with the fact that there was a 'lack of news' the first week of broadcasting, and wanted to axe the programme, but soon the show was getting seven million viewers a night. By 1988, figures had dropped considerably so ITV dropped the show, replacing it with news at 6.30 and 11, neither of which titles had quite the same ring.

On 5 March 1999, Trevor McDonald read the

News at Ten headlines for what he thought would be the last time. The news programme that followed in its wake was nicknamed the *News at When?* as ITV kept rescheduling it to fit around other programmes. It was all getting a bit ridiculous, with the *News at Ten Twenty* being introduced in 2003 and then the *News at Ten Thirty* in 2004 until Michael Grade came along and said, 'Moving the *News At Ten* to the outer reaches of the schedule was a catastrophe,' and re-established it in its rightful place in 2009, with Trevor McDonald once again at the helm.

Old Bailey

The Old Bailey – also known as Justice Hall, the Sessions House and the Central Criminal Court – took its name from the street in which it was located (which itself follows the line of the original fortified wall, or 'bailey', of the City), just off Newgate Street and next to Newgate Prison, in the western part of the City of London in the 16th century. The original medieval court was used by the Lord Mayor and Sheriffs of the City of London and Middlesex. Being near the prison was handy, for prisoners could be easily taken to and from court. The building, which stands about 200 yards northwest of St Paul's Cathedral, was first mentioned in 1585, but it burned down in the 1666 Great Fire of London, and was rebuilt in 1673. The original court had been enclosed, which led to outbreaks of typhus and the death of, among others, the Lord Mayor and two judges, and the 1673 court was built with this in mind – the courtroom was open on one side. The upper storeys were held up by doric columns, and the left out wall exposed the court to the weather. It was hoped that increased air supply would decrease the spread of disease – and it worked. The courthouse would undergo several rebuilds over the following 300 years, but the courtroom design remained essentially the same – it was laid out to emphasise the contract between the accused and the rest of the court. The defendant was positioned at 'the bar', and faced the witness box head on.

Until gas lighting became available in the early 1800s, a mirror was positioned above the bar to reflect light on to defendants' faces, which enabled the court to scrutinise any facial expressions during testimonies, and a 'sounding board' hung over their heads to amplify voices. The Central Criminal Court Act was introduced in 1856 so that cases outside of London and Middlesex could be tried here. The present building is just over a hundred years old and was built on the site of Newgate Prison. Above the main entrance is written, 'Defend the Children of the Poor & Punish the Wrongdoer'. A remnant of the old city wall, or old bailey, is preserved in the basement.

Scotland Yard

The Metropolitan Police Headquarters is actually situated at Broadway in London and nowhere near Scotland. The two men put in charge of organising the 'New Police', back in the 1830s, were Colonel Charles Rowan and Richard Mayne. They worked at 4 Whitehall Place, which backed on to Great Scotland Yard (said to have got its name from a man called Scott during the Middle Ages). At the back of the courtyard was a police station, and it's from here that the headquarters of the Metropolitan Police got its name. There are also rumours that the Kings of Scotland had resided here while in London before the Union, and that the courtyard was later used by Sir Christopher Wren. By 1887, the Police HQ included several buildings in Whitehall Place, Great Scotland Yard and Palace Place, as well as various stables and outbuildings. Headquarters were moved to Victorian Embankment in 1890, becoming New Scotland Yard, and from there to its current Westminster location in 1967.

CHAPTER SIX

FOOD & DRINK

'I'm just not keen.'

FOOD & DRINK

The 99 Ice Cream

The classic '99' ice cream cone is the taste of British summers, with its creamy vanilla ice cream, half a Cadbury flake and crunchy wafer cone. The earliest record of the ice cream was on Cadbury's price list in 1935, but the Arcari family of Edinburgh claim to have been selling 99s since the mid-1920s, and to have named them after the address of their shop at 99 Portobello High Street. A Cadbury's rep selling Flakes may have 'borrowed' the idea from Stephen Arcari, who'd set up shop in 1922.

Black Pudding

A sausage made almost entirely from congealed pig's blood in an intestine casing. Simple. What could be more delicious? Or disgusting, depending on where you place yourself in the food chain. This popular part of the full English breakfast is said to have been around as long we have been slaughtering animals and eating them. One source claims the bloody treat first appeared in ancient Greece because it is referred to in Homer's *Odyssey* as 'the roasting of stomach stuffed with blood and fat'. Wherever it came from, its popularity through the centuries has spread far and wide and it is now a delicacy in numerous European countries. And if you think our version is hard to stomach consider this: the French sometimes mix their blood up with brandy and cream. The dish has such a (perhaps surprisingly) keen following that the World Black Pudding Throwing Championships is held in Lancashire every year. The rules are simple – each contestant gets to hurl three black puddings at a giant stack of Yorkshire puddings, whoever knocks the most down wins. The tradition is said to be based on an occasion during the War of the Roses when an almighty food fight broke out due to a scarcity of ammunition.

Bovril

Popular for warming the old cockles on the football terraces, this 'beef tea' was invented in the 1870s. Napoleon's army couldn't 'march on empty stomachs' so a contract to supply one million cans of beef was awarded to the Scotsman John Lawson Johnston. But Britain didn't have enough beef, so Johnston developed a beef extract, known as Johnston's Fluid Beef. By 1888, over 3,000 pubs and grocery stores were serving the stuff, and in 1889 the Bovril Company was founded. During the Second Boer War, a similar paste was produced from horse meat and named *Chevril*. Nowadays the Malaysians stir Bovril into their coffee and porridge in the morning.

Cadbury

John Cadbury was just 22 when he opened up a grocery store next door to his father's silk and drapery shop in Bull Street, Birmingham, in 1824. He initially focused on selling mustard and hops, and cocoa and drinking chocolate were in fact only an aside! Funny when you think that Cadbury went on to become the largest confectionery manufacturer in the world. By the 1870s, business was booming and the Cadbury family bought a site in the countryside south of Birmingham called Bournville, known as 'Factory in a Garden', where they built a cocoa essence factory and a model village for their workers. By 1900, there were 313 houses set on the 330-acre estate. The family were Quakers so there were no public houses. Instead, they sold tea, coffee and cocoa as alternatives to alcohol. Cadbury launched its first milk chocolate for eating in 1897. It was created by adding dried milk powder, sugar and butter to the cocoa solids. Dairy Milk appeared on the scene in 1905, followed by Milk Tray in 1915. The company merged with JS Fry & Sons in 1919, to compete against Rowntree. In more recent years, Cadbury has merged and demerged with Schweppes, as well as buying up several chewing gum brands. As from 2009, its biggest-selling brand, Dairy Milk, is to be certified as Fairtrade in Britain. From the fluffy Cadbury Crème Eggs (*How do you eat yours?*) to the more sophisticated Milk Tray (*And all because the lady loves Milk Tray*), there's no denying Cadbury's place in the nation's collective belly.

Cheddar Cheese

Where would we be without the world-famous, good old cheddar cheese? Britain's most popular cheese is now manufactured in places as far flung as New Zealand, Canada and South Africa, but it originated in a small village in the Cheddar Gorge in Somerset. Not as old as Cheshire Cheese (referred to in the Domesday Book in 1086), but Cheddar certainly appeared as early the 12th century, when it found favour in the royal court. It is made by cutting and stacking the blocks of curd when they're still soft so that the whey can be drained off, a process known as 'cheddaring'. It is ready to eat after three months, but can be matured for up to five years. Originally, the cheese would have been made to use up excess milk, and the cool, dry Cheddar Caves were used to store and mature the cheese.

Cheddar has the advantage of being a hard cheese, which means it will keep for longer, so it was ideal for storing and would have been bought in very large quantities. Captain Scott took 3,500lbs of Cheddar with him to the Antarctic in 1901.

Cheddar was, according to Robinson Crusoe's creator, 'without all dispute, the best cheese that England affords, if not, that the whole world affords'.

It changed from being an occasional luxury to an everyday staple with the introduction of the cheese mill in the 19th century, which made production much easier.

Cheddar accounts for over half of the country's cheese market and is nowadays pasteurised, intensively farmed and produced in bulk. Fortunately, we can still take a step back in time and taste the authentic flavour of hand-cheddared cheese, in the form of West Country Farmhouse Cheddar, made using local milk in the Cheddar Gorge.

Colman's Mustard

This eye-watering yellow paste is one of Britain's most cherished brands, and without it no condiment tray would be complete. It is, along with HP Sauce and Heinz Tomato Ketchup, a kitchen cupboard staple. Colman's of Norwich dates back to 1814, a time when Wellington was preparing to defeat Napoleon at Waterloo. The all-time seal of approval came in 1866 when Colman's were granted a special royal warrant to be manufacturers to Queen Victoria. Mustard has been grown in England since Roman times, and Colman's special formula comprises two types of plant in the UK – brown mustard (*Brassica juncea*) and white mustard (*Sinapis alba*).

Colman's was very modern in its outlook, introducing contract farming in the UK, as well as being the first to build a subsidised school for its employees' children in 1864 and providing hot, affordable meals for every employee from 1868, as well as an industrial nurse to visit sick employees. So keen was the company to make Colman's a household name that the phrase 'keen as mustard' was born in the early 1900s. And what a money spinner it turned out to be. The saying goes that Colman 'made his money out of what people left on their plate', because people always take more of the potent powder from the tin than they need. Once out, it doesn't go back in. The only option of course is to buy more!

Cornish Pasty

The earliest recording of a pasty recipe is from Cornwall in 1746, though it is believed that the dish dates back a lot further than that. The Cornish pasty is made using a dense, folded pastry encasing a substantial filling of steak, onions and potatoes, and sometimes turnip, though nowadays a variety of fillings is available. The pasty was made for tin miners in Cornwall who were unable to surface for lunch, and traditionally the filling would be half sweet and half savoury, starting at one end with mince for the first course, ending up at the apple end for a bit of pudding! Their wives baked their initials into the crust, so they wouldn't get them mixed up. The idea was that they could hold the pastry by the folded crust whilst eating the rest – a whole meal in itself – and then discard the crust, which would be covered in grime and dirt from the mines anyway. Not dissimilar to today's ready meal, except that it didn't need to be reheated. In fact, the pasty could stay warm for up to ten hours, and could even help keep the miners warm if kept close to the chest. The miners were a suspicious bunch, believing that the pastry they discarded would appease the 'knockers', mischievous creatures much like leprechauns who lived in the mines. A good way to test the quality of your pasty is to drop it down a mine shaft: if it survives that, then you can be assured you've got a quality item.

Curry Houses

Britain's first 'curry' is reported to have been served in 1773 at a coffee house in Haymarket but the first eatery dedicated to Indian-style food was the Hindostanee Coffee House opened by Dean Mahomet in the West End. The word curry stems from *Kari* in Dravidian (a group of Southern Indian languages), a word meaning gravy or sauce; it doesn't refer to the spice as many people think. The first truly fashionable Indian restaurant was Veeraswamy's, opened in 1927 on Regent Street, where it still stands. The venerable act of washing our curry down with beer stems from a visit made to Veeraswamy's by the Prince of Denmark, no less. He was so impressed with the restaurant that he offered them an annual case of Carlsberg as a token of his gratitude.

The Indian restaurant trade was originally staffed by many ex-seamen from India, but by the early 1970s at least three-quarters of Indian restaurants in

Britain were owned by Pakistanis. Now over 65 per cent of Indian restaurants in the UK are run by Bangladeshis. Chicken tikka masala was invented in Britain by Bangladeshi chefs; it is quoted as being an Indian but apparently nobody in India knows about it! More than one in ten Brits make it their first choice on the menu and it has even been said to have replaced fish and chips as Britain's national dish.

Custard Cream

Ask the British public what their favourite biscuit is, and nine out of ten people will say custard cream, according to a 2007 survey of 7,000 biscuit lovers. The little biscuit sandwiches (filled with a creamy vanilla custard) have been around for over a hundred years, and the baroque swirls on the top depicting ferns are a nod to the 19th-century craze for growing ferns. Back then, the biscuits were a sign of sophistication, and their appeal has endured, though perhaps we don't think them so classy these days.

Digestive Biscuit

So called because they originally contained sodium bicarbonate (thought to have antacid properties), the digestive is a British classic. Countless millions have been dunked in cups of tea since the 1800s. McVitie

& Price's first major biscuit was the McVitie's Digestive, the first ever digestive, devised by budding new employee Alexander Grant in 1892. It was an instant hit with the public, and today over 71 million packets of chocolate digestives (first created in 1925) are gobbled up each year in the UK – that's 52 a second. In his book *Notes From a Small Island*, Bill Bryson called the wheat-based snack a British masterpiece.

Fish and Chips

What could be a more British image than eating fish and chips from a newspaper in a drizzly seaside town? Fish and chips are not a British invention, but the fish and chip shop is. Fish – usually cod or haddock deep-fried in batter – served up in paper alongside chips, generously sprinkled with salt and vinegar, first started appearing in the north of England in the 19th century. Charles Dickens mentions a 'fried fish warehouse' in *Oliver Twist*. The dish increased in popularity during the late 1800s with the advent of trawl fishing which made it a cheap and readily available food for the working classes, and it was one of the few foods not subject to rationing during the Second World War.

Now there are more than 11,500 fish and chip shops across the UK, selling more than 250 million portions of fish and chips – two million tonnes of chips – a year. That's equivalent to one in six Brits eating fish and chips at least once a week. In fact, 20 per cent of meals in Britain are bought from a fish and chip shop on Fridays (traditionally a non-meat day in the Roman Catholic calendar). One in three potatoes ends up in the fryer. And the nation's favourite accompaniment is mushy peas (or 'Yorkshire Caviar', as it's referred to in some posh restaurants). In Holyhead in North Wales, the chip shops serve 'peas water', the water strained from the mushy peas, on the side. And, if you happen to be in Scotland, why not chase it down with a deep-fried Mars Bar?

Full English Breakfast

There is nothing that sums up the British appetite more than the Full English Breakfast. 'Bacon and Eggs', as the dish was first known, became popular in the 1920s when Edward Bernays, a public relations pioneer, began heavily promoting bacon to increase sales. He executed a survey of 5,000 physicians and reported that they recommended a hearty breakfast. Meanwhile, he steered the survey results in a favourable direction for himself by organising an advertising campaign that promoted bacon and eggs as a hearty breakfast. Little is known about when and why the other familiar breakfast items (sausages, tomatoes, mushrooms, fried bread, toast, chips are optional, beans) joined the 'fry-up' but it became so popular that establishments devoted to just that were soon opening their doors, marking the birth of the modern-day 'caff' or 'Greasy Spoon'.

Heinz Beanz

Heinz Beanz were called Heinz Baked Beans until July 2008, when the name was changed in reference to the 1960s adverts featuring the slogan 'Beanz Meanz Heinz', and today the company manufacture a staggering 1.5 million cans a day.

We think of baked beans as a quintessentially British food, but Heinz began in America, their first can rolling off the production line in the 1886. The Brits loved the imported food, which initially sold as a luxury item available exclusively in Fortnum and Mason. In 1932, a 1lb can cost 5d (2p), but in 1901 they were on sale for a whopping £1.50 in today's money – the packaging was posher then. Only four people know the secret recipe of a food that was classed as 'essential' for rationing by the Ministry of Food during the Second World War, and today Heinz Beanz are a staple food in the British diet.

Hovis

The success of the British-born Hovis company came about from one rather persistent miller, Richard Smith, who was determined to exploit the nutritional richness of wheatgerm by keeping it in flour used for breadmaking. Meanwhile, other millers were extracting and discarding it because it would quickly ferment and render the flour useless. In 1886, Smith perfected his method to remove the wheatgerm, lightly toast it and put it back in the flour, keeping all the nutritional goodness along the way. It was patented in 1887, and developed as a brand by Smith and S Fitton & Sons Ltd, who milled the flour and sold it along with branded baking tins to other bakers. Thinking up an appropriate name was a bit of a challenge so it was opened out to the public in a competition to come up with the right brand. Herbert Grimes came up with Hovis from the Latin phrase *hominis vis*, meaning 'the strength of man'. Hovis were so grateful to Grimes that when he died they issued his wife with an annual payment.

The 'Boy on the Bike' advertisement for Hovis in 1973 stole the nation's heart. The ad, which was filmed on Gold Hill in Shaftesbury, was directed by Ridley Scott – of *Alien* fame – and featured Antonín

Dvořák's *Symphony No. 9*. The boy on the bike went on to become a firefighter in East Ham in 1979.

HP Sauce

Today HP Sauce is actually owned by American company Heinz and manufactured in Holland. That doesn't detract from the fact that a fry-up wouldn't be the same without it. Frederick Gibson Garton, a grocer from Nottingham, invented the recipe (made with malt vinegar and a blend of fruits and spices) and registered the name in 1896. He then sold the recipe for £150 to Edwin Moore and his Midland Vinegar Company in Birmingham to pay off an outstanding debt for malt vinegar. Oh, the irony!

After a few years getting the recipe just right, Moore went on to launch it in 1903. Garton had proudly told Moore that it was popular among the old boys in Westminster and that it had even been seen in the Houses of Parliament restaurant. For this reason, it was named with the letters HP. The bottle also bears a patriotic image of the Houses of Parliament on the label which was said to be Moore's addition to make it more marketable. Truckloads of the stuff were shipped to every corner of the British Empire. The Prime Minister Harold Wilson was so fond of smothering his food in it that it was called 'Wilson's Gravy' throughout the 1960s and 70s. 'If Harold has a fault, it is that he will drown everything with HP sauce,' his wife saucily revealed to the *Sunday Times*.

Hula Hoops

Hula Hoops, made by United Biscuit, were launched in 1973 and people have been sticking them on their fingers ever since. According to UB, 16 billion Hula Hoops are scoffed in the UK every year, a total length (if joined in a continuous tube) equivalent to going round the world four times!

Jellied Eels

Although many of us haven't actually tasted a jellied eel, they remain, nonetheless, synonymous with British cuisine. Eels became a popular dish among the poor, originating in East London in the 18th century. They were fished out of the muddy Thames estuary and then kept alive in barrels before being brought home to cook or to market to sell. Stewed in a spiced jelly (solidified fat from the eels… Mmm, nice!) and served up hot or cold, they're still to be found in traditional pie and mash shops served with 'liquor' (made from parsley, flour and eel juice!) in the East End of London and even as far afield as Essex. The oldest surviving shop is M Manze, which opened in 1891.

Jelly Babies

Everyone loves a jelly baby, and everyone has a favourite colour! One might say the jelly baby is a national institution, so it is fitting that they were invented for symbolic reasons. They were first created by one of Britain's oldest confectioners, Bassett's, to symbolise peace at the end of the First World War, and, apart from production being temporarily halted during the very un-peaceful Second World War because of rationing, they've remained a hit ever since. In 1953, the name changed from Peace Baby to Jelly Baby.

Liquorice Allsorts

In the world of inventions, the all-time favourite Bassett's Liquorice Allsorts is a great example of an accident leading to something great. According to George Bassett of Sheffield, the colourful confectionery was created in 1899 when a salesman of theirs, Charlie Thompson, went to present the Bassett's sweet portfolio to a wholesale director. Thompson was having little success until he catastrophically knocked over all his trays of sweets. Within the sugary chaos he had created were nuggets of plain black liquorice mixed in with a range of novelty coloured shapes crafted from cream paste. This was when the wholesale director became interested – he loved the contrast of all the shapes and colours and immediately placed an order with Bassett's. Liquorice Allsorts soon became a big hit. The finishing touch to a confectionery classic was added with the birth of Bertie Bassett, a little liquorice man printed on the packet, and an edible one placed inside the packet.

Marmite

It's disgusting. No, it's delicious. Whatever. It's British and it's been with us for over a hundred years. 'Love it or Hate it?' – that's what you have to ask yourself as you smear this dark-brown meaty-tasting paste on your bread. Marmite is made from brewer's yeast that has already been used to turn sugar into alcohol, a by-product that used to be thrown away. It was German scientist Justus Liebig who discovered that after, the brewing process, the yeast cells could be concentrated to yield a tasty spread. The Marmite Food Company was founded in 1902 in Burton upon Trent in a disused malthouse down the road from the Bass Brewery, the suppliers of the yeast paste. By 1907, a second factory was needed to deal with the growing demand. Marmite was basically trying to taste like beef extract, to compete with its main rival Bovril, so it could appeal to vegetarians with a blood lust. They cleverly added Vitamin B to the mix in 1912, so that the spread became even more popular during the First World War, when the vitamin B1 deficiency beri-beri was more widespread. Ex-pats are particularly fond of Marmite, for some reason. A young man kidnapped by the Kashmiri separatists in India in 1994 reached straight for a pot of Marmite on his release. 'It's just one of those things,' he said, 'you get out of the country and it's all you can think about.'

Mrs Beeton

Mrs Beeton's *Book of Household Management*, published in 1861, is one of the most famous cookery books in existence. Mrs Beeton was born Isabella Mayson on Milk Street in London in 1836, and went to school in Heidelberg, Germany. At the age of 20, she married Samuel Beeton, a book and magazine publisher. She started publishing articles on cooking and household management in her husband's magazines, writing a monthly supplement to *The Englishwoman's Domestic Magazine* in 1859–61. These were published as a single volume with the snappy title of *The Book of Household Management Comprising information for the Mistress, Housekeeper, Cook, Kitchen-Maid, Butler, Footman,*

Coachman, Valet, Upper and Under House-Maids, Lady's-Maid, Maid-of-all-Work, Laundry-Maid, Nurse and Nurse-Maid, Monthly Wet and Sick Nurses, etc. etc.—also Sanitary, Medical, & Legal Memoranda: with a History of the Origin, Properties, and Uses of all Things Connected with Home Life and Comfort. She died four years later, at the age of 28, not from exhaustion, surprisingly, but from puerperal fever, a serious form of septicaemia, following the birth of her fourth child. The book had sold nearly two million copies by 1868.

The Pint

We're talking about the popular drink here, not the fluid measurement, though if you're interested a pint is one eighth of a gallon, based on ten pounds of distilled water at 62°F. Beer was first brewed in Mesopotamia around the fifth millennium BC. It probably arrived in Britain with the Celts. Upon their arrival, the Romans noted that 'ale', comprised of barley, fermented yeast and water, was the tipple of choice among Britons. They tried growing grapes for wine but it was a waste of time. The Normans then tried to introduce cider and wine, but met with the same difficulties. By the Middle Ages, ale was the main beverage, brewed at home. The tradition of drinking imported beer goes back a long way: in the 1400s, beer, as we now know it, was introduced from Flanders and Holland. And here's where the distinction between beer and ale was born, as beer was made using hops, which gave it a bitter taste, while ale is a darker sweeter pint. Monasteries and abbeys started to brew their own, for themselves and their thirsty pilgrims, and during the Industrial Revolution major breweries took over the helm.

Nowadays multinational breweries dominate the beer industry, but there are still quite a few regional breweries, using traditional methods. Lager is the UK's most popular pint. It's just a fizzier beer ('lager' means 'storage' in German) as it's left to carbonate for longer. Twenty-six million pints are drunk every day in the UK: that's the equivalent of 99 litres per head per year. Not bad going.

Pubs

The boozer, the local, the watering hole – the national icon of British socialising – a focal point for communities in towns and villages throughout the land. The first drinking houses in this country were known as Tabernae, they arrived with the Romans and were resting places selling wine and food to exhausted troops. Pub signs had not yet been invented but large vine bunches were suspended from the Tabernae to indicate the nature of their trade. The Romans left in the fifth century AD and public use of Tabernaes dropped off, replaced by home brewing for some time. The oldest pub, although many lay claim to this, is recorded in the *Guinness Book of Records* as 'Ye Olde Fighting Cocks Inn' in St Albans, Hertfordshire, with its foundations dating back to 793 AD.

Roast Beef and Yorkshire Pudding

Since Elizabethan times, Englishmen and beef have gone together like Frenchmen and brie. Even the royal bodyguards are known as Beefeaters, mainly because of the amount of meat they put away. It was noted in 1719 that 'it is common practice, even among People of Good Substance, to have a huge Piece of Roast-Beef on Sundays, of which they stuff until they can swallow no more, and eat the rest cold, without any other Victuals, the other six Days of the Week'. Indeed, village squires would reward their serfs for their six days' hard labour by roasting an oxon on a spit. Beef was the meat of the well-to-do, while the plebs ate bacon (or went vegetarian). The novelist Henry Fielding's song 'The Roast Beef of Old England' was a huge hit in the 1700s. In 1748, William Hogarth painted *The Gate Of Calais*, better known as *The Roast Beef Of Old England*, featuring a rib of beef being delivered to an English hotel in Calais. Is it any wonder the Brits are referred to as *le Rosbif* by their Gallic friends? Hogarth was one of the founding members of the Sublime Society of Steaks, who met weekly in Covent Garden to gorge themselves on grilled sirloins. Throughout the Second World War, the Brits had to make do with bully beef, an inferior canned variety. Roast beef's traditional accompaniment, Yorkshire Pudding – or Dripping Pudding, as it would have been known then – used to be placed under the spit roast to soak up the drippings, and was used as a filler for people who couldn't afford much meat. The first recorded recipe was in *The Whole Duty of a Woman* in 1737.

Spotted Dick

First referred to in Alexis Soyer's 1850 book *The Modern Housewife of Menagere*, spotted dick has become a classic British dessert made from suet pastry and dried currants. But why the name? The spotted bit is easy – the currants constitute the spots on the pudding. But the dick bit is a little more puzzling. It is certainly not a rude reference to the male anatomy, and it has been suggested that the word is a corruption of the last past of 'pudding' (i.e. puddick). Whatever the truth, it remains a popular treat, and is usually served with a good portion of custard.

Tea

Tea was created more than 5,000 years ago in China and has been Britain's most popular drink since the middle of the 18th century, when it replaced ale and gin as the masses' favourite tipple. It was brought to England by East India Company traders in 1664 and was first sold at Thomas Garaway's London coffee house in Exchange Alley in 1657. Over 100 million cups of tea are consumed every day in the UK; 96 per cent of it is brewed from tea bags, and 98 per cent of people take their tea with milk. Afternoon tea is a fine British custom, which consists of a spread of sandwiches, scones (or 'cream tea', with butter, jam and clotted cream) and cakes, traditionally served on a tiered stand, all accompanied by freshly brewed tea. It was Catherine of Braganza, Charles II's Portuguese wife, who popularised the taking of tea in the afternoon. Nowadays, with everyone so busy, afternoon tea is a rare treat. But fortunately we've managed to hang on to the 'tea break'.

Wine Gums

Who, as a child, didn't wonder why wine gums are called wine gums? After all, they're not made of wine, and they don't taste of wine. The truth is nobody is quite sure why Charles Gordon Maynard, son and employee of Libyan sweet-shop owner Charles Riley Maynard, decided on that name for the sweets he had created. What we do know is that when he presented the wine gums to his father in 1909 he nearly got the sack, for Daddy was a strict Methodist and teetotaller. Charles set about convincing him that his recipe did not contain a drop of wine and production finally went ahead. It had been said that the idea for the name came from its creator's perception that the colours of the gums in some way related to different colours of wine. Beyond question, though, is the success of the product. In 1990, Trebor Bassett took over Maynard's, and the sales figures for Maynard's wine gums reached £40 million for 2002. Children's writer Roald Dahl was a massive fan, and he kept a jar of them by his bed so he could enjoy a couple each night before he drifted off. Perhaps they offered some kind of inspiration for one of the greatest characters in the sweet world, Willy Wonka.

CHAPTER SEVEN

THIS SPORTING LIFE AND LEISURE

THIS SPORTING LIFE
AND LEISURE

Bingo

No British town would be complete without a bingo hall brimming with the elderly armed with black marker pens and a good ear for bingo caller's rhymes. Its origins stem back to 16th-century Italy where a state-run lottery game played en masse, a direct ancestor of bingo as we know it today, was invented. A French derivative of the Italian version named Lotto was enjoyed by 17th-century French noblemen before bingo spread throughout Europe in its several different forms. It has even been used as a mathematical aid in schools, a practice which originated in Germany. In 1920s America, Beano as it was then known was being played with beans. It is claimed that, in a fit of excitement over winning, a player called out 'Bean-go' instead of bingo, and so came the name that stuck. By the 1950s, Catholic churches and working men's clubs were popular bingo venues, with the police turning a blind eye in most cases. Miss World competition founder Eric Morley introduced bingo as a pastime in the UK. Morley used it as a way to fill large spaces such as cinemas and dance halls that had fallen into disuse after television was introduced. Morley then turned existing Mecca dance halls into bingo halls and launched the hugely successful Mecca Bingo Company which is still going strong today. The introduction of commercial bingo did bring concern though, and a spate of complaints included headlines such as 'Bingo's hold on womenfolk' and 'Wife's bingo led to divorce'. It didn't stop the rapid increase of bingo fanatics across the country.

Butlins

Butlins holiday camps have been entertaining families for over 70 years and they are an intrinsic part of Britain's modern history. Born in South Africa in 1899, Billy Butlin is the man who brought a bit of Hi-de-Hi! to some of the nation's most popular leisure spots. Butlin had been working on travelling fun fairs and had already been thinking about setting up something fun-fair related. Another ingredient to his winning holiday brand came about when he noted the custom of landladies throwing out their guests between meals, regardless of the weather. He wanted to open a fun holiday camp with a philosophy of welcoming and entertaining families round the clock. Butlin opened his first camp in 1936 in Skegness, and an advertisement in the *Daily Express* offered three meals a day and free entertainment. Another camp followed two years later, and another the year after that. The camps were used as military bases throughout the Second World War, but post-war Britain saw a boom in interest, with holidays in Butlins costing as little as a week's pay. And so the empire grew with William Butlin being knighted in 1964. The business was sold to the Rank Organisation in 1972 for £43 million.

Car Boot Sales

No doubt car boot sales have grown out of a long tradition of market trading in the UK. The market hall was central to civic pride in Victorian Britain. Spurred on by the entrepreneurial spirit of the Eighties and with attics and garages full of Rubik's Cubes and BMXs, it was time to get rid of all the tat accumulated over generations. And so the car boot sale was born. It's not clear when the first boot fair actually took place, although we do know that the term was coined in September 1980 by Barry Peverett, who had organised a boot sale at his farm in Wrotham Heath, Kent. Eager to pique people's curiosity, he came up with 'boot sale' which seemed to do the trick. The name stuck, and carbooting became a nationwide obsession on Sundays.

Cricket

The fact that we're not so good at the sport doesn't mean cricket isn't wholly British. *Chamber's Dictionary of Etymology* states that the word cricket, borrowed from *criquet*, means a goalpost in a game of bowls, or that it may have come from *cricke*, middle Dutch for stick or staff. There is little information about how cricket came about but a mass of information, much of it anecdotal, suggests it was invented by children in a dense woodland in southeast England called the Weald in the 1500s.

Working-class men are said to have taken up with the sport sometime later before the upper classes did the same in the 1600s, around Sussex and Kent. Large crowds flocked to matches at the Artillery Grounds in London from 1730, and the first cricket club was formed at Hambledon, Hampshire, in the

1760s. Sponsored by wealthy patrons, with members including local tradesmen and farmers, the club established techniques of batting and bowling which still hold today. The Marylebone Cricket Club was founded in 1787 by Thomas Lord. The first grounds were at Dorset Square in London, before they moved to St John's Wood. Lord's laid down the formal laws of the game, and an annual match called 'Gentlemen vs. Players' took place at the grounds from 1806 to 1963, featuring the amateur 'gentlemen' from schools and universities, against their semi-professional counterparts, the 'players'. Cricket quickly spread to the colonies: the first overseas tour was in America in 1862. Rivalry between Britain and Australia lead to the formation of The Ashes in 1882. Cricket requires patience, though, as some matches can last as long as five days. Indeed, Lord Mancroft is quoted as saying, 'Cricket is a game which the British, not being a spiritual people, had to invent in order to have some concept of eternity.'

Croquet
A quintessentially English lawn game that involves hitting wooden or plastic balls through hoops with a mallet, croquet took England by storm in the

1860s. There are several theories about its origins: one being that it was introduced to Britain from France during Charles II's reign and was called Paille Maille, meaning 'ball and mallet' in Latin. The overriding theory is that it arrived from Ireland, via Brittany, around 1851. A certain Miss MacNaghten, who observed peasants in Ireland playing the game, passed on the details to Isaac Spratt, a toy maker on Brook Street in London, who then went on to make some sets, print the rules and put the game on sale. Mr Spratt sold his interest to John Jacques, of the manufacturer Jacques of London, who later claimed to have recorded the rules himself after watching the game being played in Ireland. He published his first *Laws and Regulations* in 1864 and played a unique role in popularising the game in the UK, although the fact that it could be played by men and women caused some controversy. By the late 1870s, tennis had taken over in the popularity stakes, and many of the croquet clubs, including the All England Club at Wimbledon, converted their lawns to tennis courts. The manufacturing of croquet equipment has been passed down through the generations at Jacques of London, the oldest sports and games manufacturer in the world.

Crufts

The annual breed show for perfect pooches has been held every year since 1891. Its founder, Charles Cruft, turned down a position in the family jewellery business to work as an office boy in a shop in Holborn selling dog biscuits. Charles went on to become a travelling salesman, coming into contact with many sporting kennels throughout the land. He travelled to France in 1878, where French dog breeders invited him to organise the promotion of the canine section of the Paris Exhibition. Eight years after that he was managing the Allied Terrier Club Show at the Royal Aquarium, Westminster, and there was no stopping him. The first Crufts show took place in the Royal Agricultural Hall in Islington in 1891, and Charles made a tidy profit. After his death in 1938, his widow took over but she found it all a bit too much, so she handed the reins over to the Kennel Club. They held their first show, which was a huge success, at the Olympia in London in 1948. Nowadays it's a Brummy affair, since the centenary show was held at the Birmingham National Exhibition Centre in 1991.

Darts

The popular pub game of darts began in Medieval England, when soldiers used empty upended wine barrels for target practice with shortened arrows. It's believed that the young soldiers took their arrows with them to local pubs to show off their newly honed skills. Once they'd drunk all the wine and used up all the barrels, it was up to some bright spark to invent a new dartboard, this time a cross-section of a moderate-sized tree. The board would have had rings, of course, and as it dried out sections would have naturally formed. It wasn't long before woodworkers were supplementing their bar tabs by fashioning dart boards for their local watering holes. Henry VIII was a big fan of the game and received a beautifully ornate dart set from his second wife, Anne Boleyn. The game of darts as we know it today wasn't fully formed until around 1900. The numbering layout was devised by Brian Gamlin just 14 years earlier, and it was only in the early part of the 20th century that the 'clock' board became standard. The favourite darting catchphrase, *One hundred and eighty!*, can be heard in pubs up and down the land. It's not clear when the current fashion for shiny shirts and beer bellies originated.

Football

The beautiful game of English soccer is one of many variations of football played around the world. The ancient Egyptians certainly enjoyed a game, perhaps as a fun way of tilling the soil. Greeks and Romans played a variation with the catchy name of *phaininda*, while the Chinese, who began playing back in the 3rd century BC, had already professionalised it under the name *cuju* or 'kick ball' by the 7th century. Shrovetide football matches were popular in England during the Middle Ages. 'Mob football' was played between neighbouring towns and villages, with unlimited numbers of players struggling to move an inflated pig's bladder to a delegated place on their opponents' land. The 'pitches' effectively included streets and village greens. They were particularly violent affairs, with people and property being frequently injured. The Lord Mayor of London banned football 'on pain of imprisonment' in 1314, for causing 'great noise in the city … from which many evils might arise'. Interest in the sport didn't dwindle, however, and King Henry VIII himself ordered a pair of football boots in 1526. Women's football was played from the 1500s, as noted by the poet Sir Philip Sidney. Public schools are commended with taking football away from the 'mobs' and turning it into an organised team sport.

The Football Association met at the Freemasons' Tavern on Great Queen Street, London, for the first time in October 1863. The FA Cup was established in 1871. These days more people watch the World Cup than any other sporting event in the world.

Golf

All you need is a club and a ball and you're away! It's no wonder some form or other of this gentle stick-and-ball sport has been played since earliest times. A popular theory is that it began with stones being hit around rabbit runs where the Royal and Ancient Golf Club in St Andrews now stands. It is believed that golf is borrowed from *colve*, a middle Dutch word for bat or stick used in a ball game. Throughout Europe in the Middle Ages, variants of golf were played, sometimes teeing off at one village and putting in the next. 'Goff' was enjoyed by kings and commoners alike in the 15th century. An Act of Parliament had to be brought in to restrict the playing of 'gowf' in Scotland so that archery wouldn't be forgotten. It was along the links of Scotland's east coast that the game, played with a cleek and ball made of leather and stuffed with chicken or goose feathers, developed into modern-day golf. Golf clubs started to spring up from the late 1700s, and Allan Robertson, of the famous ball-making family in St Andrews, was the first golf professional. The 'gutta percha' ball or gutty, made from the evaporated sap of a tree commonly found in Malaysia, was discovered in 1848, transforming the game for good. Iron clubs could now be used for driving, lofting, jiggering and putting. The first purpose-built golf course was created in 1851 on the links of Monkton parish in Prestwick, and the first Open Championship was held there nine years later, with a first prize of a red leather belt from Morocco.

Morris Dancing

These stick-toting, handkerchief-waving folk dancers are emblematic of Britain's folk-music tradition. Morris dancing officially dates back to the 15th century, and may have its roots in rites celebrating fertility and the coming of spring. Dancers used to blacken their faces with soot so they'd resemble Moors and not be recognised by the local priest, hence the name 'Moorish dauncers'. Some believe the dance was brought back from Spain around 1387 by John of Gaunt, the second son of Edward III. By the 1500s, morris dancing had been assimilated by the Church and was performed for Easter, Whitsuntide and saints' days. In 1600, the out-of-work Shakespearean actor William Kempe morris danced from London to Norwich for a wager, an event chronicled in his book *Nine Daies Wonder*. Morris dancing declined throughout the 17th and 18th centuries but was rescued from obscurity by a few English folklorists, such as Cecil Sharp and Mary Neal (a suffragette and social reformer), who set about collecting and recording dances and songs from all over the country.

Royal Ascot

The English knights returning from the Crusades in the 12th century brought Arab horses with them. These horses were bred with our own to produce the thoroughbred horses used in racing today. In the 17th century, Charles II held horse races on private courses or open fields, with Newmarket as the first horseracing meeting venue. While out riding in 1711, Queen Anne came across an open heath at East Cote near Windsor Castle that looked like an ideal place for 'horses to gallop at full stretch'. The first race meeting took place there that year, on 11 August. The first event, Her Majesty's Plate, was worth 100 guineas and was open to any horse over the age of six. These horses were built for stamina (they would have been English Hunters) as they had to carry a weight of 12 stone and race in separate heats which were each four miles long. The racecourse was laid out by William Lowen and the first permanent building was erected in 1794. After that, an Act of Enclosure passed by Parliament in 1813 ensured that Ascot Heath would be kept as a racecourse for the public. The first four-day meeting took place in 1768, and the Gold Cup was introduced in 1807, paving the way for the millinery madness of 'Ladies Day'.

Rugby

According to Rugby School, the 16-year-old student William Webb Ellis, 'with a fine disregard for the rules of football ... first took the ball into his arms and ran with it, thus originating the distinctive feature of the rugby game.' Ellis, who went on to be an Anglican clergyman, had no say in the matter as he died two years before this was publicised. There was even talk that he'd been doing nothing more than giving a demonstration of an ancient Irish sport called *caid*, which he would have witnessed as a child while his father was stationed in Ireland. Whatever the truth, the Rugby students went out and spread the good news and by 1839 the first team at Cambridge was established, along with the 'Cambridge Rules'.

In 1871, the Rugby Football Union was founded in a London hostelry and that same year Scotland beat England in the first ever international. A year later, the first Varsity match was held between

Oxford and Cambridge. The International Championship followed soon after, as did the first British Lions tour to Australia and New Zealand, and by 1895 the labouring northerners had broken away from their toff southern counterparts over pay disputes for loss of working hours to create the Northern Union, which would become Rugby League. France was welcomed into the International Championship in 1910, forming the Five Nations, but they were thrown out again (briefly) for carrying stiletto knives in their socks. The first World Cup was hosted by Australia and New Zealand in 1987, and the cup was named after our old friend, William Webb Ellis.

Snooker

We have one man to thank for the naming of the game: Colonel Sir Neville Chamberlain (no relation to the former Prime Minister). While playing a colourful version of the gambling game, black pool, he accused a young opponent of being 'a regular snooker' when he missed a pot. In 1875, a snooker was a first-year cadet at the Royal Military Academy. Chamberlain was gentlemanly about the whole thing, though, saying they were all 'snookers' to the game, and the name was adopted for the pastime. Sir Neville went off to join the Central India Horse in 1876, taking the game with him. After being wounded in the Afghan War, he moved to Ooatacamund, where the game became the speciality of the 'Ooty Club', with rules being posted in the billiards room. John Roberts (Junior), who was then Billiards Champion in the UK, met Chamberlain in 1885, while dining with the Maharajah of Cooch Behar. Old Neville, being the good sport he was, passed on the rules of snooker to Roberts, who brought it back to England with him, and by the turn of the century the game had caught on in a big way. Rules that had been drafted and recorded were finally recognised by the Billiards Association – the governing body of the time – in 1900. Snooker eventually took over from English billiards as the dominant cue sport in the 1930s when the legendary Joe Davis actively promoted the game throughout the world.

Wimbledon

Wimbledon is the oldest tennis tournament in the world and has been held at the All England Lawn Tennis and Croquet Club since 1877. The club was founded in 1868 as the All England Croquet Club, and was situated off Worple Road, Wimbledon. Lawn tennis was invented by Major Walter Clopton

Wingfield in 1875 (its original name – Sphairistike – was a bit of a mouthful and didn't catch on). It became a fixture at the All England Club in 1877, and the first Lawn Tennis Championship was held to mark its arrival. The Gentlemen's Singles, which was the only event held that year, was won by Spencer Gore, an old Harrovian rackets player, and watched by 200 spectators who'd paid one shilling each. The principal court was situated in the middle, with the other courts arranged around it, hence the title 'Centre Court'. Ladies' Singles arrived on court in 1884. Gentlemen's Doubles were introduced that same year, followed by Ladies' Doubles and Mixed Doubles in 1913. The reigning champion only had to play in the final, but that all changed after 1922, when the grounds moved to a large new stadium on Church Road. By the turn of the 20th century, Wimbledon had a worldwide reputation. During the Second World War, the club had a farmyard and was used by the ambulance services, Home Guard and a decontamination unit. A bomb struck Centre Court in 1940, resulting in the loss of 1,200 seats. Virginia Wade was the last Briton to win the Ladies' Singles event, back in 1977. And, even further back, Fred Perry was the last Briton to win the Men's Singles, in 1936 – a year before the Championship was first televised, unfortunately.

CHAPTER EIGHT

ARTS AND ENTERTAINMENT

'The author of James Bond and his
creation may have needed penicillin but
he did not discover it.'

ARTS AND ENTERTAINMENT

Alfred Hitchcock

The suspense films and psychological thrillers of Alfred Hitchcock have been a staple of British cinema since the late 1920s. Born in East London in 1899, and named after his greengrocer dad, Alfred endured a childhood that was far from ideal. According to the director, his early years were lonely, miserable and sheltered, blighted by his obesity. Alfred's parents were another source of unhappiness. His father often sent his young son to the local police station with a note asking them to put him away for misbehaving, while his mother would make him stand at the foot of her bed for hours at a time. Hardly idyllic, but all good material for the creation of the Norman Bates character in *Psycho*, made in 1960 and considered to be one of the great man's finest films.

Hitchcock graduated as a draftsman and advertising designer, and created title cards for silent movies before directing his first movie – *Number 13* – in 1922. *Number 13* certainly proved unlucky for this film, which was cancelled mid-production, and the scenes that had been shot were lost. Undeterred, Alfred went on to make his first thriller, *The Lodger: A Story of the London Fog*. Released in 1926, it was a huge success. From then on, it was onwards and upwards, although his first Hollywood movie, *Rebecca* (1940), was his only film to win an Academy Award for Best Picture, despite the later success of classics such as *Vertigo*, *Rear Window* and *The Birds*. With cameo appearances in his own films and the long-running TV series *Alfred Hitchcock Presents* (1955), Hitchcock became a celebrity famed for his droll voice and wry humour. The director was once quoted as saying, 'Actors are cattle,' although he later clarified the point: 'Actors should be *treated* like cattle,' he reflected.

The Archers

First advertised as 'an everyday story of country folk', BBC Radio 4's *The Archers* is the longest-running radio soap in the world. Set in the fictional village of Ambridge in fictional Borsetshire, the action centred around the Archer family, owners of Brookfield Farm. The series was created by Godfrey Baseley, a producer of farming programmes for radio, and written by Geoffrey Webb and Edward J Mason. After a successful broadcast to the Midlands as a pilot series on Whit Monday 1950, the soap truly got going on 1 January 1951, after which five 15-minute episodes were transmitted weekly across the country. In fact, the series was so successful that at one stage 60 per cent of the population was tuning in. These were the post-war years of rationing and food shortages, so the Ministry of Agriculture got in on the act, with *The Archers* acting as a kind of educational conduit for farmers and smallholders to encourage them to increase their productivity.

Such is its popularity that there have been many cameo appearances over the years – Princess Margaret appeared with the Duke of Westminster in 1984 as part of the NSPCC's centenary commemoration; Judi Dench broke the silence of character Pru Forrest in 1989 to celebrate episode 10,000, and Alan Titchmarsh judged the Ambridge gardening competition in 2003.

To date, more than 15,800 episodes have graced

the airwaves, and the show still has over one million faithful listeners.

Banksy

Banksy's identity is one of Britain's best-kept secrets. With fans like Brad Pitt and Angelina Jolie, it's a wonder this anonymous graffiti artist can bear to stay hidden. The search for his identity has led the British press on a wild goose chase, but we still can't be sure who he is. He may, in fact, not exist at all but be an art collective. Or he may be Peter Gunningham, who was born in Bristol in 1973 and attended the private Bristol Cathedral School, where former pupils claimed he was a gifted artist who just 'disappeared' after leaving home. The Gunninghams say it's a load of nonsense, but the rumours are still flying around. The other theory is that he was born in 1974, raised in Yate, near Bristol and trained as a butcher. Graffiti really took off in Bristol in the late 1980s, and it's believed the young meat cleaver got caught up in the excitement. Others, still, say his real name's Robert Banks and that he learned his craft spray-painting his way through an unhappy adolescence and designing bootleg rock memorabilia. This Banksy served time for petty crime. Whoever he is, this Artful Dodger has a taste for the illicit as well as the aesthetic. As he says himself, 'Art should have your pulse racing, your palms clammy with nerves and the excitement of creating something truly original in a dangerous environment.'

British Museum

Over 250 years old, the British Museum is the nation's very own treasure trove. The Ulster-Scot physician and naturalist Sir Hans Sloane, who also gave his name to Sloane Square in London and introduced drinking chocolate to England from Jamaica, was a great collector – mainly of books, natural specimens and some antiquities, such as medals and coins. When he died in 1753, he bequeathed over 71,000 objects to King George II and the British people in exchange for a payment of £20,000 to his estate. An Act of Parliament in the same year established the British Museum to house the artefacts. In 1757, King George II added the 'Old Royal Library' of the sovereigns of England to the collection, and the museum opened to the public on 15 January 1759. Its first home was Montagu House in Bloomsbury, and all 'studious and curious Persons' were given free entry. Some of its most famous – and controversial (countries want them back!) – artefacts include the Elgin Marbles, a set of classical Greek marble sculptures, and items relating to ancient King of Egypt Tutankhamen, all acquired in the 19th century. The natural history collections were moved to South Kensington in the 1880s and became the foundation of the Natural History Museum, while the book collection became the cornerstone of the British Library in 1973. The museum was hit twice during the Second World War, the second bomb passing through the hole made by the first and neither of them exploding.

There is always plenty to see, and, if Tutankhamen doesn't float your boat, the loaves of bread that are over 5,000 years old just might.

Bruce Forsyth

The king of light entertainment was born in London in 1928 to a family who owned a car-repair garage, but Bruce had no intention of becoming a mechanic. Inspired by Fred Astaire, he trained in dance and appeared on a talent show on TV, probably an episode of *Come and Be Televised*, when he was only eight years old. At 14, Brucie made his first professional outing in show business with an act called 'Boy Bruce, the Mighty Atom' – a song and dance act involving an accordion – and was soon doing pantomimes and circuses. His strong-man act went down well (and is probably where the

'Thinker' pose he made famous originated), but fame was still a long way off. Bruce toiled for years before getting his big break, and it was his stint as the presenter of *Val Parnell's Sunday Night at the London Palladium* from 1958 to 1960 that set the world ablaze and finally made Brucie a household name. The *Generation Game* followed, and the rest is history. Many gameshows later – remember *You Bet* and *The Price Is Right?* – and Brucie had become something of a national treasure. He was awarded an OBE in 2006. In 2007, the great British public voted his 'Nice to see you, to see you, nice' catchphrase as the most popular in the UK.

Carry On Films

Cheap, sexist, seaside-postcard farcical, slapstick and innuendo-packed, *Carry On* films sum up an era of British humour at its best (or worst, depending on your point of view). The first of these most English of comedy capers was *Carry On Sergeant* shot in 1958 starring Bob Monkhouse and William Hartnell (who went on to be the first Doctor Who). The film was supposed to be a straight adaptation of the war stories of RF Delderfield, but director Gerald Thomas thought it would be more fun to go down the comedy route. Thomas had entered the film industry and worked with such stellar talent as Orson Welles and Laurence Olivier, but *Carry On Sergeant* was the film that led him astray. He went on to make 29 films almost entirely in Pinewood Studios.

The films' producer, Peter Rogers, was notoriously tight-fisted, and leading actors were paid a paltry £5,000 per picture from 1958 up until the late Seventies – a fact lamented by Kenneth Williams in his diaries – and the ladies were paid even less than the men. Budgets were tight elsewhere too. For *Carry On Cleo*, the crew used the leftover sets from *Cleopatra*, the very film it was parodying, with Sid James helping himself to Richard Burton's costume. Rich and Liz Taylor weren't the only ones miffed. Marks & Spencer found little to laugh about when they found out that two characters were called Marcus and Spencius. *Carry On Camping* was filmed one cold British autumn, so leaves were painted green and glued back on to the trees. The famous scene where Barbara Windsor's bra flies off was created using a fishing rod to whisk it through the air.

That said, with their archetypal British characters and the double dose of double entendres, they're the most successful series of British films ever made.

Charlie Chaplin

Known affectionately to millions as the Little Tramp, Charlie Chaplin had endured a rather Dickensian childhood which prepared him well for the part. He was born in London in 1889 to music-hall entertainers. His mother was in and out of asylums, and his father, who deserted the family when Charlie was three, eventually died of alcoholism. One of Charlie's earliest performances was at the age of five, when his mother was booed off the stage and he came on to take her place, singing 'Jack Jones'. Charlie and his brother were left in workhouses and orphanages at a young age, and by ten Charlie had left school and was working as a mime on the vaudeville circuit. He made his first trip to America in 1910, with Fred Karno's Speechless Comedians. His first film, *Making a Living*, in 1914, was a big success and by 1916 he was demanding a weekly salary of $10,000, making him one of the highest-paid people in the world.

'Chaplinitis' had well and truly taken hold by 1920. Admirers included such luminaries as George Bernard Shaw, Sigmund Freud and Marcel Proust, and he became an icon of the Beat Generation in the 1950s, with Jack Kerouac wanting to go on the road and be a hobo like The Tramp.

Far from his humble beginnings, Chaplin controlled every aspect of the filmmaking process, founding United Artists and producing, casting and directing the films he starred in.

Coronation Street

Mother of all TV soaps, Corrie has graced our screens since 1960. The show was created by a relatively inexperienced scriptwriter called Tony Warren for Granada TV. The working title of the Manchester-based show was *Florizel Street*. It was Agnes, a tea lady at Granada, pointed out that 'Florizel' sounded like a kind of disinfectant. The execs went with *Coronation Street* in the end, with *Jubilee Street* coming a close second.

Having written 13 episodes at first, Tony Warren thought that would be it. How wrong he was. Initially aired on Monday nights at 7.30, the show was immensely popular for a decade until a second weekly slot was introduced in the 1970s, and a third in 1989. Tony managed to take time out, however, to help write the Beatles-inspired film *Ferry Cross the Mersey* in 1965, before retiring in 1968.

Three of the original cast remained with the show for 20-odd years: busybody Ena Sharples, the tart with a heart Elsie Tanner and snooty landlady of the

Rovers Return Annie Walker. Ken Barlow is the only remaining character from the original episode. Barlow, who has been married four times, divorced and widowed twice, has had four children and 27 girlfriends, and has still had time to be a teacher, newspaper editor, community activist and supermarket trolley-boy.

The unmistakable cornet piece used for the show's theme tune was composed by Eric Spear – who received £6 for his efforts.

Commenting on the first episode in 1960, the *Daily Mirror* opined, 'The programme is doomed from the outset... For there is little reality in this new serial, which apparently, we have to suffer twice a week.' Realistic or not, *Coronation Street* remains the most popular British soap of all time.

Costume Dramas

Blushing maidens, stern old widows, gallant gentlemen, courtly manners and passionate yearning – the Brits can't seem to get enough of the costume drama. Part of British cinema since the silent era, 'period' dramas have been around since the 1930s, and are now a regular fixture on our TV screens. During the Second World War, the Ministry of Information encouraged filmmakers to emphasise Britain's heritage and history by producing gung-ho movies celebrating British military might, but studios took a more intellectual approach from the late 1940s, producing such classics as *Oliver Twist* and *Anna Karenina*. The 1950s saw Oscar Wilde's *The Importance of Being Earnest* brought to the big screen, while *Tom Jones* and *Lawrence of Arabia* were phenomenal successes in the 1960s. Serial dramas arrived on our screens in the 1970s, with the likes of *Women in Love* and *Murder on the Orient Express*. In 1981 *Chariots of Fire* – a true story about two athletes competing in the 1924 Olympics – renewed the world's faith in British cinema. Merchant Ivory went on to produce many successful 'heritage' films, such as *Howard's End* and *A Room with a View* (both EM Forster novels) and *Remains of the Day*, adapted from a novel by Kazuo Ishiguro, bringing actors like Emma Thompson and Julian Sands world fame.

Since then there have been a spate of adaptations of Jane Austen and Emily Bronte novels, most notably *Pride and Prejudice*, featuring *that scene* where Colin Firth walks dripping from the lake, further arousing the nation's interest in romantic literature.

Doctor Who

Who is Doctor Who? Who knows who he is, but he's travelled through time and space, and back again to be with us. But how did the show come about? In 1962, the BBC needed some family entertainment to fit between *Grandstand* and *Juke Box Jury* on Saturday nights, and looked to Canadian head of drama Sydney Newman for an answer. A big science-fiction fan, Sydney looked to the galaxies and got together with some of the BBC's scriptwriters to bash out some ideas. Their initial concept was a tad vague: a time machine and a central character known only as the 'Doctor'. But they ran with the idea and Anthony Coburn soon penned the first episode, which led children to believe that an innocent-looking police box could be a time-travelling tardis. *Doctor Who* was meant to be an educational show, but the Beeb soon realised they couldn't afford to dress the tardis up to look like a sarcophagus in Egypt, so they scrapped that idea. The Doctor and his cohorts began their time-travelling adventure on 23 November 1963, voyaging 100,000 years into the earth's past to help a caveman discover fire. Sparks flew, and our hero (played by ten different actors to date) continued to fight off Daleks and right wrongs for 26 series from November 1963 until December 1989.

After a rather long break, the series returned in 2005, written by Russell T Davies, and has been prime-time viewing ever since, making *Doctor Who* the longest-running sci-fi show in the world, a fact that would make Mary Whitehouse turn in her grave. Everybody's favourite moral crusader made repeated complaints to the BBC throughout the 1970s – she didn't like the gore and was scared by the Daleks – but viewing only rose each time she complained.

Edinburgh Festival Fringe

More commonly known as The Fringe, the alternative to the Edinburgh International Festival is today the largest arts festival in the world. But, as you'd expect from an event with 'fringe' in the title, the roots of the event are humble. It all began in 1947 when eight theatre groups turned up uninvited to the first Edinburgh International Festival. These daring troupes wanted to take advantage of the large crowds of luvvies looking to lap up a heady mix of classical music, opera, dance and theatre, so stationed themselves on the outskirts of official proceedings and performed away. 'The Fringe' was so named the following year by the Scottish playwright Robert Kemp who observed that, 'Round the fringe of official festival drama, there seems to be more private enterprise than before.'

Things soon snowballed. Before long, thousands of performers were arriving in Edinburgh each year, and the unofficial Fringe was soon rivalling the official festival. In 1958, the Festival Fringe Society was formed to provide information, a central box office and a published programme. To this day, the fringe is an 'unjuried festival' – anyone is free to perform if they want to. And, in three no-holds-barred weeks in August, when Edinburgh welcomes everyone from street performers to some of the biggest names in showbiz, ticket sales add up to around £1.5 million a year from over 2,000 shows in 250 venues.

The Hay Wain

Dusty old prints of John Constable's painting of a hay wain – a horse-drawn cart – on the River Stour in Suffolk can be seen in houses and inns across the country. The painting didn't cause much of a stir when it was first exhibited at the Royal Academy in 1821, under the title *Landscape: Noon*. The French, however, didn't miss a trick, and Charles X of France awarded it a gold medal, a cast of which can be seen in the picture's frame. Constable's father owned Flatford Mill, just upstream from this particular scene, and the house on the left bank was rented by a local farmer by the name of Willy Lott. It still stands there today. Constable painted *The Hay Wain* indoors, in his London studio, working from a series of sketches. 'When I sit down to make a sketch from nature, the first thing I try to do is to forget that I have ever seen a picture,' Constable once said. Bizarrely, he died from acute indigestion.

James Bond

007 has been donning his tux and drinking his martinis 'shaken not stirred' since the 1960s. Bond, an officer of the British Intelligence Service (MI6), was created by Ian Fleming while on holiday at Goldeneye – his Jamaican estate – in 1952. Bond, who was named after the ornithologist and author of *Birds of the West Indies*, bears an uncanny resemblance to his creator. Ian Fleming worked as a British spy while covering news for *The Times* in Russia, and joined the British Naval Intelligence during the Second World War, heading a secret commando squadron. Like Fleming, 007's father is Scottish (his mother would have been too, had the author not been inspired to base her on his Swiss fiancée at the time), and both character and creator attended the same schools and had a penchant for scrambled eggs, booze and beautiful women.

Fleming's first novel, *Casino Royale*, partly inspired

by his experience in the Naval Intelligence Division, was published in 1953 by Jonathan Cape. Of the 4,728 copies printed, half were given to public libraries. Not a great start, but Fleming went on to publish 12 novels and a short-story collection between 1953 and 1964, and, in 2006, first editions of *Casino Royale* were selling for up to £40,000. Needless to say, it was the Bond films that helped turn Fleming's fortunes around. The first Bond movie – *Dr. No*, directed by Terence Young, and starring Sean Connery and Ursula Andress – was released in 1962, accompanied by the iconic 'James Bond Theme', composed by Monty Norman and orchestrated by the John Barry Orchestra. The film was a huge success, and the rest, as they say, is history.

There have, of course, been many Bonds, the most famous being Connery and Roger Moore. The adventures of the Aston Martin-driving international playboy continue to capture the heart of a nation, and 007 is still going strong, with twenty-two films to date and Daniel Craig currently flying the flag for Her Majesty's Secret Service.

Madame Tussauds
Thanks to Madame Tussauds, holiday snapshots the world over feature smiling starstruck tourists standing

next to their waxwork heroes. Marie Tussaud was taught the art of wax modelling in Paris by Dr Philippe Curius, for whom she did some housekeeping in return. The first wax figure Tussaud created was of Voltaire. Other people she modelled include Rousseau and Benjamin Franklin, as well as many prominent victims of the French Revolution (she searched for their heads among the corpses). Tussaud inherited a vast collection of wax models after the doctor's death and spent 33 years travelling around Europe with them, before arriving in London in 1802 only to find herself unable to return home because of the Franco-British War. Her collection was displayed at the Lyceum Theatre for a while, and briefly at the Baker Street Bazaar, before moving to its current location on Marylebone Road in 1884. One of the main attractions was the Chamber of Horrors, which featured her French Revolution grotesques. Fire damage in 1925, followed by the Blitz, meant that most of the 400 models were destroyed, although the casts survived. Tussauds was sold to a group of businessmen in 1889, and the crowds have never stopped coming. There have been some controversial figures at Madame Tussauds: a model of Hitler, unveiled in 1933, had to be replaced in 1936 and kept under close guard after being continually vandalised.

A self-portrait of Madame Tussaud, who died in 1850, is on display at the entrance to the museum. Of the thousands of celebs, sports stars, politicians, musicians and actors who've been immortalised in wax, only one person has ever declined the offer to be modelled: Bollywood actor Aamir Khan. The reason? He didn't want to feel 'special'.

Sir Michael Caine

Better known to his family as Maurice Joseph Micklewhite, Caine was born in South London in 1933. His dad was a fish-market porter, his mum a charwoman, and life wasn't easy at first. Lack of finances meant the young Maurice suffered vitamin deficiency in the womb and was born with rickets. Once he was old enough to walk, Maurice's ankles couldn't support his weight and he was forced to wear surgical boots. If that wasn't tough enough, his ears protruded badly and for two years his mother would stick them back with plasters – as a result, his ears grew so close to his head that for the rest of his life Michael has been slightly deaf. Michael left school at 16 to pursue a career in acting before doing national service from 1951 to 1953 in Germany and Korea. He met his first wife at the Lowestoft Repertory and they moved to London.

But the marriage quickly fell apart, and two years later Maurice found himself at home with his ailing father, working in a steel yard. After his father died, he decided to seek his fortune in Paris, but ended up working in a snack bar. Still, Michael kept on with his dream of acting, and eventually landed himself a bit part in *A Hill in Korea*, but the film didn't bring him instant fame. Years later, on the verge of giving up acting altogether, his agent got him a job on TV in a play called *The Lark*. 'Maurice' changed his name to Michael Caine, after the film *The Caine Mutiny*, which was showing at the time.

By the end of the 1950s, even the Chief Casting Director at Associated British Pictures was advising him to give up acting. But this just made him more determined and, by 1963, after years of treading the boards and living hand to mouth, he got a part in the movie *Zulu*, and then along came *The Ipcress File*, *Alfie*, *The Italian Job*, *Get Carter* – the list goes on and on. In short, Michael Caine is a living legend, but he still uses his real name when not working – and not a lot of people know that.

Monty Python
The Pythons – five Oxbridge graduates (John Cleese, Graham Chapman, Terry Jones, Michael

Palin and Eric Idle) and Terry Gilliam, an animator from Minneapolis – created what has come to be regarded as one of the most influential comedy sketch shows in the world. Having made their bones at the Oxford Revue and Cambridge University Footlights, as well as writing and performing on shows like *That Was the Week that Was* and *The Frost Report* (with David Frost), they were well equipped to take the nation by storm. *Monty Python's Flying Circus*, later known simply as *Monty Python*, was broadcast on the BBC from 1969 to 1974. The opening sketch on the first show featured a farmer who believed his sheep were birds and nested in trees, and the public were hooked. After the success of their comedy show, they went on to create such classic movies as *The Life of Brian* and *Monty Python and the Holy Grail*. Three of the six members – Palin, Idle and Cleese – were recently voted by fellow comedians to be among the top 50 greatest comedians ever. Graham Chapman, who was also a qualified doctor, was the first to say 'shit' on British TV. After *Monty Python*, John Cleese, whose surname originally was 'Cheese', went on to create *Fawlty Towers*; Terry Gilliam is now a successful film director; Eric Idle co-wrote the award-winning West End musical *Spamalot*; Terry Jones writes history books; and Michael Palin is a

147

modern-day Phileas Fogg. So popular is their brand of absurdist comedy that the word 'Pythonesque' has entered the English lexicon.

Pantomime

The panto is nowadays the place British pop and soap opera stars retreat to after they've done their stint on TV – oh yes it is. But this hasn't always been the case. The word *pantomimos* means 'imitate all' and comes from Greece. The first pantomime in England, called *A New and Dramatick Entertainment of Dancing after the Manner of Ancient Pantomimes called the Loves of Mars and Venus*, was staged at the Theatre Royal on Drury Lane in 1717. It was the actor John Rich who popularised this low form of opera in the 1750s, with the scenes growing ever wilder over the next 50 years, until Joe Grimaldi arrived as Clown in 1800. Strings of sausages began appearing on stage, and by the mid-1800s the stories of Cinderella, Jack and the Beanstalk et al were commonplace, and were part of the 'traditional' Christmas reverie. Lucy Vestris became the first female principal to cross-dress in pantomime around 1830 and in 1902 Dan Leno took the part of Mother Goose. The pantomime dame was born, paving the way for the likes of Les Dawson and Danny la Rue.

Rolf Harris

So he isn't technically British, but Rolf is so heartily loved in UK that he truly belongs in this book. The entertainer's parents were born in Cardiff in Wales, but Rolf was born in Perth, Australia in 1930. A champion swimmer and, at 14, the youngest artist to have a self-portrait hung in the prestigious Archibald Prize, he enrolled at the City & Guilds School in London in 1952 and showed paintings in the Royal Academy Exhibition for two years running. Rolf was drawn back to Australia in 1960 to star in children's TV, but he didn't stay away for long. By 1967, he was back on British TV with *The Rolf Harris Show*, which ran for seven years and made famous his catchphrase, 'Can you guess what it is yet?' His song 'Tie Me Kangaroo Down, Sport' was a hit in 1960, with 'Sun Arise' and 'Two Little Boys' following hot on its heels. Rolf is famous for using a 'wobble board' in his songs. Rolf's board is made of thin hardboard, and he discovered the 'instrument' by chance while preparing to paint conjurer Robert Harbin's portrait on hardboard back in 1959. Before Harbin showed up, Rolf had prepared the board by covering it with oil paint and turpentine and, after drying it over a paraffin heater, he burned his hand. I'll let Rolf tell the rest of the story: 'I propped it between the palms of my hands and shook it to cool it down. And I thought, What a marvellous sound. The rest is history.'

It was Rolf who taught the 1980s generation to draw in *Cartoon Time* and *Rolf's Cartoon Club* on ITV. Since then he's been doing various odd jobs, including presenting *Animal Hospital* and painting the Queen's 80th birthday portrait.

Tabloid Newspapers

Beloved of the Brits, the tabloid newspaper is a concise publication with tongue-in-cheek headlines, juicy gossip and sensational stories about everything from sleazy politicians to celebrities. In the 1800s, Burroughs, Wellcome & Co., a London-based pharmaceutical company, introduced 'tabloid' pills, which compressed the usual bulky medicinal powders into tiny capsules. The term was brought into popular use to refer to anything that was 'compressed', from whence came the phrase 'tabloid journalism' in 1901, in reference to the papers' condensed stories. It was only in 1918 that tabloid newspapers actually took on their diminutive size – their page dimensions are approximately 17 by 11 inches. The *Daily Mail*, first published by Alfred Harmsworth in 1896, is Britain's oldest tabloid newspaper. The paper's owner sent a telegram to Hitler on 1 October 1938 in support of Germany's invasion of the Sudetenland, and expressing the hope that 'Adolf the Great' would become a popular figure in Britain. The *Sun*, launched in 1964, with its infamous Page Three Girl, has the highest circulation of any English-language daily in the world, at around three million, though sales have been falling of late due to the proliferation of free newspapers in cities nationwide. The *Sun*, *Daily Star*, *Daily Sport* and *Daily Mirror*, or 'red top' papers, have more sensationalist leanings. The 'gutter press', as it's often affectionately known, is traditionally willing to pay for a good story, making them the first port of call for desperate celebrities and wannabes – so you know who to turn to if you want to dish the dirt.

Tate Modern

London's Tate Modern – also known as the Cathedral of Cool, owing to its vast space – is the place to go if you fancy a piece of Picasso or a slice of Warhol. The gallery's home, Bankside Power Station, was designed by Sir Giles Gilbert Scott – the same guy who designed Battersea Power Station and the red telephone box – and built between 1947 and 1963 on the site of an old coal-fired power station opposite St Paul's Cathedral and beside the Globe Theatre. It closed only 18 years later. Tate Britain, meanwhile, which had opened in 1897 on the site of an old penitentiary, could no longer house all of its work, so the search began to find a new space for its international modern and contemporary art collection. The Bankside Power Station was perfect, though it needed some work. The young Swiss architects Herzog and de Meuron were drafted in, and the Tate opened its doors to the public four years later, on 11 May 2000, followed a month later by the famous wobbly Millennium Bridge.

Turner Prize

Named after JMW Turner, this annual prize of £40,000 for British achievement in the visual arts has attracted some controversy over the years. It was established in 1984 by the Patrons of New Art, who were founded two years earlier as part of the Friends of the Tate Gallery to encourage the collection of contemporary art. To begin with, it was a prize for 'the greatest contribution to art in Britain in the previous 12 months' and was open to critics and art administrators as well as artists, but since 1991 the remit has narrowed to British artists under 50 who have had 'an outstanding exhibition or other presentation of their work' in the past year. Wall Street investment firm Drexel Burnham Lambert was the original sponsor, but they went bust in 1990 and the prize was suspended that year. Since then the prize has been sponsored by Channel 4, which broadcasts the award ceremony live from Tate Britain. The jury is made up of a select group of art-world insiders and has been criticised over the years – especially from the 'anti-anti art' group, the Stuckists – for choosing the most pretentious conceptual art around. Winners include Antony Gormley, Rachel Whiteread and Steve McQueen. Brian Sewell of the *Evening Standard* had this to say about the prize: 'The annual farce of the Turner Prize is now as inevitable in November as is the pantomime at Christmas.'

West End Theatre

Few would argue that London is the theatre capital of the world. The West End – Theatreland – is where it all happens. The first playhouse in London was built at Shoreditch in 1576 and was imaginatively called 'The Theatre'. When the lease ran out in 1597, its owner Richard Burbage (a friend and colleague of Shakespeare's) transported its timber across the Thames and used it to build the first Globe Theatre on the South Bank, which opened its doors in 1599. Before this, plays had been performed in courtyards, inns and people's homes. The first West End theatre opened in 1663, playing host to some of the earliest stars before it was destroyed by a fire in 1672. The Theatre Royal in Drury Lane, designed by Christopher Wren, was opened on the same site in 1674. In the 19th century, theatregoing became very popular among the middle and upper classes, and many of the theatre buildings standing today were erected during this period, with Shaftesbury Avenue, the backbone of the West End, coming into its own towards the end of the century. Agatha Christie's *The Mousetrap* is the world's longest-running production and the likes of *Les Miserables* (the West End's longest-running musical), *Phantom of the Opera*, *Chicago* and *Mamma Mia!*, to name but a few, all draw huge crowds every year. In 2007, total ticket sales exceeded 13 million, rather impressive for the 40 or so theatres within The Strand, to the south, Oxford Street to the north, Regent Street to the west and Kingsway to the east.

CHAPTER NINE
SARTORIAL MATTERS

'We turned down their application
for a grant last week.'

SARTORIAL MATTERS

Barbour Jacket

John Barbour was raised on a farm in Scotland and knew the perils of outdoor pursuits in a country like ours. This indestructible wax jacket has been with us since the 1890s. Shortly after Barbour crossed the border to work as a travelling draper, he set up Barbour & Sons, in South Shields, a coastal town in the northeast of England. Still going strong across four generations, Barbour & Sons remains a family business, Over the years, the shop specialised in all manner of outdoor wear including boiler suits, painter's jackets and oilskins designed to protect ship owners, ship builders and seamen against foul weather. John Barbour made a terrific success of his enterprise and passed it down to two of his 11 offspring, Jack and Malcolm. Malcolm expanded the sale of oilskins and began marketing to farmers and shepherds. By 1917, Barbour were receiving mail-order catalogue orders from as far off as Chile and Hong Kong. Lady Diana and her Sloane Ranger friends popularised the jacket in the 1980s, in much the same way as the Sex Pistols popularised safety pins.

Bowler Hat

OK, so you're more likely to see a woman in Bolivia wearing one of these, but they're still one of the first things that spring to mind when you think of Britain. This hard felt hat with a rounded crown was created in 1849 by the milliners Thomas and William Bowler, to fulfil an order for Lock & Co. of St James's, established in 1676 and still in business today. It's believed that the younger brother of the Second Earl of Leicester, Edward Coke, had put in the request for a hat that would protect his gamekeepers from low-hanging branches while on horseback, and possibly from poachers too. Top hats were proving to be impractical. Coke apparently placed the bowler on the floor and stomped on it to test its strength. Having passed the test, he paid his 12 shillings for it and left. The hat was then called the 'Coke', after the customer who had ordered it, as was customary. It went on to be known as the 'Billy Coke' or Billycock' in Norfolk, as it was believed it was named after the Earl's nephew, William, and not Edward. Its popularity peaked towards the end of the 19th century, offering, as it did, a sensible middle ground between the top hat, worn by the upper classes, and the flat cap, worn by the working classes. It was British railway workers who introduced the bowler to Bolivia and Peru, where they are still worn by Quechua and Aymara women.

Harrods

Brompton Road's luxurious department store had humble beginnings as a wholesale grocery store in Stepney, East London in 1834. Owned by Charles Henry Harrod, it moved to its current location in 1849 to avail of new customers on their way to the Great Exhibition of 1851 in Hyde Park. They employed two assistants and a messenger boy, but by 1880 it was a thriving store, employing 100 staff and selling everything from fruit and veg to perfume. The store burned to the ground three years later, just before Christmas, but Harrod's son, Charles Digby managed to fulfil all their deliveries and make a record profit. A new grander store was built, whose customers included Lilly Langtry and Oscar Wilde. The Harrod family sold up in 1889 and became a public company. Harrods had the world's first escalator installed in 1898, with brandy at the top to revive customers. By 1905, the building as we know it was complete. Noel Coward once bought an alligator for Christmas here, Alfred Hitchcock had fresh herrings flown to him in Hollywood, and the original Winnie-the-Pooh was found in the toy department by AA Milne. The store made yachts to order, ran a funeral service (embalming Sigmund Freud) and sold aeroplanes. It was even possible to hire a fully equipped ambulance, complete with a nurse. Lancaster bombers were kitted out with uniforms and parachutes from Harrods during the war. James Bond (Pierce Brosnan, actually) worked on the pharmacy counter in the 1970s, while Darth Vader (Dave Prowse) worked as a fitness consultant, so you were in pretty safe hands. The company was bought by the Fayed family in the 1980s.

Kate Moss
Supermodel and international fashion icon, Katherine Ann Moss was born in Croydon, London on 16 January 1974. She attended Ridgeway

Primary School and Riddlesdown High School in Surrey. Kate was spotted in JFK Airport by Sarah Doukas, founder of Storm Model Management, on her way home from a holiday in Jamaica at just 14 years old. A year later, she appeared in photo spread 'The Third Summer of Love' in *The Face* magazine. The supermodels of the 1990s were all tall and curvaceous, while Moss was a mere 5ft 6", and a waifish size 6. There was an outcry against the new 'heroin chic', with even the President of the United States, Bill Clinton, wading in.

A gold statue of the fashion icon – the largest since the time of the Egyptian Pharaohs – was created in 2008 by Marc Quinn. The artist described Moss as 'the ideal beauty of the moment'. Kate Moss without a doubt remains a truly British icon and a supermodel with huge international influence. She's not only smart but she's also versatile – Kate Moss has clothes labels and perfumes, she is a businesswoman involved in a range of different companies and she even made a guest appearance in Black Adder as Maid Marian for Comic Relief.

Kilt

This knee-length plaid garment, pleated at the rear, and traditionally worn without underpants, originated in the Scottish Highlands in the 16th century. Originally the Scottish Gaels and the Irish would have worn the same clothes, namely shirts known in Gaelic as *léines* and semi-circular mantles known as *brats*. From the 'big wrap', or belted plaid of the 16th century, whose upper half could be draped over the shoulder, evolved the 'little wrap' in the early 18th century. The English ironmaster Thomas Rawlinson is credited with its invention. Apparently, he thought the littler kilt would be more practical for the Highlanders working in his furnaces near Inverness (probably safer not to wear underpants too, in case they caught light). The Diskilting Act was brought in after the Jacobite Uprising and the defeat of Bonnie Prince Charlie in 1746, in a campaign to defrock those savage Scots. Only the armed forces were allowed to carry on wearing theirs, and it wasn't until 1782 that the Act was repealed, by which time they'd gone out of fashion. But fashions come around again, and by 1822 King George IV was visiting Edinburgh kitted out in the full Highland dress. Queen Victoria decorated rooms in Balmoral Castle with tartan, and was fond of wearing it herself, sparking a worldwide trend.

Marks & Spencer

Marks & Sparks has long been a leading store on British high streets. Michael Marks was born in Slonim, Russia, in 1859, to Polish refugees. He emigrated to Leeds as a young man, where he found employment with the sympathetic warehouse owner, Isaac Dewhurst. Marks opened his own penny bazaar stall at Kirkgate Market in Leeds in 1884. Shortly afterwards, he opened a shop at 20 Cheetham Hill Road, Manchester, together with a Yorkshire man, Tom Spencer. Another shop followed shortly after, in Cross Arcade, Leeds. By 1897, they had 36 branches and a new warehouse in Manchester. Spencer died when he was only 53, while Marks died two years later at the age of 48. The business grew into a retail empire under Michael's son Simon, who was chairman until 1964. Marks & Spencer became a limited company in 1926 and the famous St Michael trademark appeared in 1928, with food and canned goods following three years later.

Miniskirt

One of the enduring emblems of London in the 'swinging sixties', the decade-defining miniskirt was the outrageous fashion item that caused a sensation on the international fashion scene. They were first seen in 1964 as part of designer André Courrèges's collection and they hit Britain in 1965 when Mary Quant, an über-cool London designer, began selling skirts that were 6in (15cm) short of the knee, which she named after her favourite Mini Metro. London was well and truly swinging. Fashions come and go, but the miniskirt has become something of a staple in every fashion victim's wardrobe, thanks to Quant. Born in London in 1934, the young Quant spent her childhood ransacking crashed warplanes with her brother. 'Our prize possession was some poor pilot's thumb,' she noted. She was drawn to dressmaking at an early age, using nail scissors on one occasion to cut up her bedspread. She managed to secure a scholarship to Goldsmith's Art College, where she met her future husband, with whom she eventually set up shop on the Kings Road. The shop was called Bazaar and was an instant hit with the Chelsea set. 'It was no wonder we did such a roaring trade the moment we opened,' she later wrote. Their mark-up on their clothes was much smaller than in any other shop, and they were actually taking a loss on some items, unbeknownst to themselves.

Twiggy

Nowadays she's a busy TV presenter, mum, animal rights activist and M&S model, but back in the swinging sixties she was a stick-thin teenager with a boyish mod cut and painted-on eyelashes. Born Lesley Hornby in the London suburb of Neasden in 1949, she went to school in Kilburn and was nicknamed Twiggy as a child. She got her first job in the hairdressers where her sister worked, and then went on to work on the counter at Woolworths and at a printing firm. She was sweet 16 when she was offered her first modelling contract, and she weighed just 6 1/2 stone. 'It's not what you'd call a figure, is it?' was Twiggy's line. Soon she was being booked by *Elle* and *Vogue* and would become Britain's first supermodel. The *Daily Express* named her the 'face of 66'. The philosopher Marshall McLuhan commented in 1967, 'Twiggy is an X-ray, not a picture.' Diets soon became all the rage.

Vivienne Westwood

It's Vivienne Westwood we have to thank for bondage gear and pins as a fashion item. Born Vivienne Isabel Swire to a shoemaker and cotton weaver in Glossop, Derbyshire in 1941, she moved with her family to London when she was 17 and attended Harrow Art School for just one term. At 21, she married Derek Westwood and became a primary school teacher, and they had a son together. After that, she met 18-year-old Malcolm Edwards (aka McLaren), with whom she had a second son. She and Malcolm opened a shop in 1971 called 'Let It Rock' on the Kings Road, which went through various names, including 'Too Fast to Live, Too Young to Die' and 'SEX'. They were fined for 'exposing to public view an indecent exhibition' in 1975 and of course this is where the Sex Pistols famously started out. All this time, Westwood was selling her outrageous designs in the shop and creating a huge following. By 1984, she was working with Giorgio Armani. Five years later, she was ranked as one of the world's top six designers, became Professor of Fashion at Vienna Academy of Applied Arts and married one of her students. In her own words, 'Fashion is about eventually being naked.'

Wellington Boots
This fashionable waterproof footwear was first made popular by the Duke of Wellington in the 18th century. The Duke of Wellington, an Anglo-Irish soldier and statesman, commanded the Allied army that defeated Napoleon at the Battle of Waterloo.

He went on to be Prime Minister from 1828–30, and briefly again in 1834. Wellington, who was commander-in-chief of the British Army until his death in 1852, had his shoemaker modify the then popular Hessian boot, standard issue among the military and used widely by civilians too. The new boot was made with soft calfskin leather so it was comfortable as well as tough and hard-wearing. The boot's popularity quickly gained ground, as young gentlemen endeavoured to emulate this war hero.

Hiram Hutchinson first started manufacturing rubber boots in France in 1853, after buying the patent from Charles Goodyear for vulcanised natural rubber. Over a million pairs of wellies were made by the North British Rubber Company during the First World War, to keep soldiers' feet dry in the trenches. By the end of the Second World War, the Wellington boot's popularity was widespread. The cowboy boot is also an offspring of the Hessian boot, making it a close relative of the wellie.

Wellie wanging, in which participants have to hurl wellies as far as they can, is a bizarre but popular sport in the UK. The origins of the sport are unclear, but historians are fairly sure it has nothing to do with Napoleonic Wars!

CHAPTER TEN
MUSIC

'…and for my 12,307th choice, I'd have the live extended version of…'

MUSIC

Andrew Lloyd Webber

The man who gave us *Jesus Christ Superstar*, *Cats*, *Evita* and many more besides was born into a musical family in 1948 – his father was a composer and his mother was a pianist and violinist. Andrew had his first suite published at the age of nine, and liked to put on 'productions' with his brother Julian, now a famous violinist, and his aunt Viola in his toy theatre. His aunt, who was an actress, took him backstage at many of her shows, which ignited his love of theatre. Lloyd Webber claims to have set music to TS Eliot's *Old Possum's Book of Practical Cats* at the age of 14. He was a Queen's Scholar at Westminster School and studied history for a time at

Oxford, before transferring to the Royal College of Music to pursue his interest in musical theatre. Lloyd Webber collaborated with Tim Rice from the mid-Sixties, producing some of his most memorable musicals. The duo wrote a song for the Eurovision Song Contest called 'Try It and See' but the British decided not to. The tune was turned into 'King Herod's Song' instead. Lloyd Webber's second wife, Sarah Brightman, was cast as the lead in *The Phantom of the Opera* (now the second-longest-running West End musical in history and the longest-running Broadway musical).

Andrew's mantelpiece must be a little crowded, as he has won seven Tony Awards, three Grammies, an Academy Award, seven Olivier Awards and a Golden Globe. And don't forget he's the man who wrote 'Memory', 'I Don't Know How to Love Him' and 'Don't Cry For Me, Argentina', surely, some of the best karaoke classics of all time.

Bagpipes

The bagpipes are like the lungs of Scotland. The funny thing is, though, they're not actually Scottish in origin but Middle Eastern, dating back to before the birth of Christ. Back then, they would have been made up of a bit of old goatskin and some reeds, which were gradually replaced with the hollowed leg bones of small animals, with holes drilled into them to vary tone and pitch. The Greek playwright Aristophanes wrote 'pipe with your bone flutes into a dog's rump' in 425 BC. The Romans brought the pipes to Britain, along with straight roads, and they became hugely popular in Scotland and Ireland: by the 14th century the strain of the pipes could be heard in nearly every village. Bagpipes were used to rally the clans to battle, as well as to mourn the passing warriors. The English tried to ban the Scots and the Irish playing them, but that didn't stop them. By the time of the two world wars, the Highland regiments were rallying the troops with the Scottish Great Highland Bagpipe and their popularity soared.

The Beatles

In 1957, the 17-year-old John Lennon formed a skiffle group called The Black Jacks with his best mate Pete Shotten (on the washboard) and a few other lads. A week later, the band became The Quarry Men, named after their school, Quarry Bank High. They were playing at an annual garden festival at St Peter's Parish Church in Woolton when they were introduced to Paul McCartney. Paul picked up a guitar and started playing one of Lennon's favourites, 'Twenty Flight

Rock'. Lennon was bowled over – not least because Paul could remember all the words, something John struggled with. A few weeks later, Paul was in. In February 1958, Paul's 14-year-old friend George Harrison joined the group. By November 1959, they'd changed their name again, this time to Johnny and the Moondogs. The group recorded their first songs, 'That'll Be The Day' and 'In Spite of All the Danger', which weren't released until after the break-up of The Beatles. While working at the Fox and Hounds Bar in Caversham, John and Paul were brought up to play a few tunes and introduced as The Nerk Twins. But by May 1960 the band – which now consisted of John, Paul, George and Stuart Sutcliffe, a friend of John's – were calling themselves The Beatals, inspired by Buddy Holly's Crickets and the Beats. A month later, they finally settled on The Beatles. The 'fifth Beatle', Stuart Sutcliffe, died of a brain haemorrhage two years later, and The Beatles went on to find their final member, Ringo Starr. The Beatles made their first appearance at Liverpool's Cavern Club in February 1961, and made nearly 300 appearances there before the release of their first studio album *Please Please Me* in 1963. Beatlemania was around the corner, and four decades on record sales had exceeded one billion copies internationally.

Brass Bands

In the Middle Ages, 'Waits' – members of night watches who patrolled the streets and walls and guarded the gates of towns and cities – would stand next to soldiers on watch all over Britain and herald danger on their trumpets, horns or sackbuts. Town bands, adopting the term, developed outside the courts from the 16th century onwards and played dances such as *Allemandes* and *Sarabandes*, imported from the French and Italian court. By the early 1800s, brass bands, had become popular among the working classes. Factories were good places for such music to thrive, with some employers even funding instruments and providing practice space – the bands were thought to keep the men away from more dubious pastimes. Cynical factory owners were not interested in the music, but believed funding bands and providing transport to and from competitions and practices would keep their workers from engaging in Trade Union disputes (they also used the bands to advertise their businesses locally). Despite this, some bands – such as the Black Dyke Mills from Yorkshire – became more successful than the companies they represented. Working conditions had greatly improved by the 1860s, so that the working classes had more spare time to pursue their love of brass. Not such good news for the likes of the British conductor, Thomas Beecham, who was quoted as saying, 'Brass bands are all very well in their place – outdoors and several miles away.'

BRIT Awards

The country's premier music awards began in 1977 under the auspices of the British Phonographic Industry, which still dishes out the award for Outstanding Contribution to British Music. The first show was held at Wembley Conference Centre and, as a way of marking the Queen's Silver Jubilee, honoured the best in popular music over the previous 25 years. Winners included Cliff Richard, The Beatles and Simon & Garfunkel, while Procol Harum was the first band to perform, with 'Whiter Shade of Pale'. It should probably have been renamed the Robbie Williams Awards – the cheeky chappie has performed more than anyone else, been nominated for more awards and won more awards than any other performer in the history of the show.

Desert Island Discs

Desert Island Discs has whisked us off to a fictional island every week on BBC Radio 4 for over 60 years. Devised by Radio Presenter Roy Plomley, the show's format is simple. Each week, a guest is interviewed and chooses eight songs – along with one book and one luxury item (they are automatically given *The Complete Works of Shakespeare* and the Bible, or any other appropriate religious book) – to take with them when cast away on an island. The first of a series of eight weekly programmes was broadcast in January 1942 from a bomb-damaged studio in Maida Vale, featuring the first ever guest, American comedian Vic Oliver. Plomley went on to present 1,791 editions of the programme over 43 years. Michael Parkinson was his successor for a relatively short three years, before Sue Lawley was stranded on the island for 18 years. She has now been replaced by the delectable Kirsty Young. Plomley went on to host *One Minute Please*, which later became *Just a Minute*, and he was awarded an OBE in 1975.

Some of the luxury items guests have requested include marijuana, a blow-up doll and a cat. The most requested music is 'Ode to Joy' by Beethoven, and the last six prime ministers have all been castaways.

Glastonbury Festival

The largest open-air music festival in the world began as the Pilton Festival, at Worthy Farm in the

Vale of Avalon. Glastonbury Festivals – a series of classical concerts, lectures and recitals – had been taking place in the town of Glastonbury since 1914, always attracting a bohemian crowd. This new festival began on 19 September 1970, the day after Jimi Hendrix died, and was attended by 1,500 people. It went on for two days, featuring acts like Al Stewart and T. Rex. The entry fee, which included free milk from the farm, was £1. Its organiser, Michael Eavis, had been inspired by an open-air Led Zeppelin concert at the Bath Festival of Blues and Progressive Music. The following year, the date was moved to the summer solstice and it was renamed the Glastonbury Fayre. Entrance was free and the first pyramid stage was erected, built on a site above the Glastonbury-Stonehenge ley line. Acts included David Bowie, Joan Baez and Fairport Convention. The next festival kicked off seven years later, in 1978, and was a small event with around 500 people. It wasn't until the 1980s that Michael Eavis made the festival an annual fixture, creating a permanent pyramid stage that doubled as a cowshed in winter. The crowd limit was set at 30,000 back in 1983, but has since grown to over 100,000, and the site moved to Cockmill Farm in 1985 as Worthy Farm was just too small.

National Anthem

'God Save the Queen' (or 'King', as it would have been then) became popular at the height of Bonnie Prince Charlie's fame in the late 18th century. It first appeared in print in 1744 in the anthology *Thesaurus Musicus*, with the words appearing in the *Gentleman's Magazine* a year later. The origin of the tune is shrouded in myth and hearsay, although it bears some similarities to an early plainsong (traditional Roman Catholic church songs) melody, as well as to a keyboard piece written by John Bull in 1619. It was first performed in the Drury Lane Theatre in 1745, and the following year George Frideric Handel used the tune in his *Occasional Oratorio*, an ode to the Jacobite Rebellion of 1745. Various composers used it as a point of British reference thereafter, including Ludwig von Beethoven. Nowadays it's most likely to be heard in football stadiums throughout the land and at the close of Radio 4 each night at 12.59pm.

Proms

Britain's finest classical music festival runs from mid-July to mid-September every year, attracting huge audiences from across the country. Prom is short for 'Promenade Concert', which simply means a show where part of the audience stands in the 'promenade' area of the hall (in front of the stage). The first Proms concert was back in August 1895 and was devised by Robert Newman, manager of Queen's Hall in London. Newman offered Henry Wood conductorship of a permanent orchestra, and of the first Proms season, and their aim was to popularise classical music by creating an informal atmosphere with low ticket prices (5p for a single concert or £1.05 for a season ticket). In the early days, the festival was known as 'Mr Robert Newman's Promenade Concerts' and the programmes lasted around three hours. Eating, drinking and smoking were allowed, and the second half was generally shorter and lighter, featuring the Grand Fantasia – a selection from the most popular operas at the time. Monday night became 'Wagner night', while Fridays were reserved for Beethoven. Many of the leading composers of the day were introduced to the audience, including Strauss, Debussy and Rachmaninov. The BBC took over the Proms in the 1920s, and the BBC Symphony Orchestra was formed in 1930. Once in the hands of the Beeb, concerts could be broadcast to a much wider audience.

On 10 May 1941, the Queen's Hall was gutted by a Luftwaffe bombing raid and the Proms were moved to the Royal Albert Hall, where it has remained ever since. The festival now includes over 70 main concerts every year, and every Prom is broadcast live on BBC Radio 3. And then there's the last night, a classical knees-up of popular tunes, patriotic songs and flag waving on the second Saturday of September. Tickets for the concert – which always includes the classics 'Land of Hope and Glory', 'Rule Britannia' and 'Jerusalem – are highly sought after.

The Rolling Stones

The Rolling Stones were the bad boys' answer to The Beatles. Mick Jagger and Keith Richards met at primary school and a decade later the two shared a mutual friend in musician Dick Taylor and jammed together in their band Little Boy Blue and the Blue Boys. Meanwhile, multi-instrumentalist Brian Jones had fathered two illegitimate children by the age of 16 and drifted to London where he played with Alexis Korner's Blues, Inc. Jones began jamming with Jagger and Richards while working at the Ealing Blues Club. The trio, along with drummer Tony Chapman, cut a demo tape that was rejected by EMI. The band changed its name from Blues, Inc. to The Rolling Stones, after a Muddy Waters song, and had their first gig in July 1962. By 1963, Bill

Wyman and Charlie Watts had joined them and their first single 'Come On' reached No. 21 in the charts. That same year, their song '(I Can't Get No) Satisfaction' stayed at No. 1 for four weeks and catapulted them into the pop stratosphere.

The Sex Pistols

Johnny Rotten walked into Vivienne Westwood and Malcolm McLaren's boutique on the Kings Road one day in 1975, wearing a homemade 'I Hate Pink Floyd' T-shirt. McLaren was looking for a lead singer for the band he was managing at the time, and asked him to audition by singing along to Alice Cooper's 'Eighteen' on the jukebox. His tone-deafness was ignored, and so the Sex Pistols was formed. After just a handful of performances, the group signed to EMI for a very large advance, and their first single, 'Anarchy in the UK', was released just in time for Christmas 1976. During an interview with Bill Grundy on the *Today* programme – as last-minute replacements for Queen, no less – the band used a whole host of expletives that caused a hullabaloo in the British press, with the *Daily Mirror* famously running the headline 'The Filth and the Fury!' Most of their concerts were cancelled or erupted into violence on their Anarchy Tour, and the band was duly dumped by EMI. Matlock was allegedly kicked out of the Pistols for 'liking The Beatles', and was replaced by Rotten's friend Sid Vicious, who couldn't play at all but looked the part. In May 1977, the band was signed with Virgin, and they released the single 'God Save the Queen', which was banned by the BBC and others but still managed to shoot up the charts. The US tour that followed lasted only 14 days and the band fell apart, with Johnny Rotten's final utterance on stage being, 'Ever get the feeling you've been cheated?'

Tom Jones

Welsh sex-bomb Tom Jones was born Thomas Jones Woodward in Cardiff in 1940. As a young lad, he'd regularly sing at family gatherings, weddings and his mother's Women's Guild meetings. But he wasn't so popular in the school choir, as he used to drown out everyone else. As a teenager, Tom was a bit of rebel without a cause, playing truant, drinking and chasing girls about south Wales, but a bout of tuberculosis put an end to all that – as he was forced to stay in bed for a year. But he made up for lost time once he was better, leaving school at 16 and becoming a husband and dad by the age of 17. Tom worked at a paper mill for a while before becoming frontman for Tommy Scott and the Senators in 1963. The band made a demo tape in 1964 but couldn't get a record deal in London, so they returned to Wales with their tails between their legs.

Just when it seemed all over, Tom was spotted one night by a London-based manager called Gordon Mills. 'The first few bars were all I needed to hear,' Mills later said. 'They convinced me that here was a voice that could make him the greatest singer in the world.' Mills renamed the singer and took Tom Jones back to London with him and recorded his first single, 'Chills and Fever', in 1964. That was a bit of a damp squib, but the following single, 'It's Not Unusual', was an instant smash hit, and Tom was soon on stage dodging more knickers than he'd had hot dinners. The pants throwers kept it up for decades, but eventually Tom complained it was all a bit much. 'I want it to end now because it has lost all its meaning,' he told the *Sun* in 2005. 'If I'm doing a ballad and trying to create a mood, then undies appear from nowhere, it's a problem.'

CHAPTER ELEVEN

LANGUAGE AND LITERATURE

'This one was hatched within the
sound of Bow bells.'

LANGUAGE AND LITERATURE

Agatha Christie

Agatha Christie is the bestselling mystery writer of all time. She has sold four billion books, which her estate claims puts her behind only Shakespeare and the Bible. Christie penned 69 mystery novels and her play, *The Mousetrap*, has been running in London's West End since 1952. The beloved 'Queen of Crime', Agatha (nee Miller) was born in Torquay in Devon in 1890 and raised by her aunt until she married Archibald Christie, an aviator in the Royal Flying Corps, in 1914. Agatha wrote her first book as the result of a challenge from her sister Madge and, once written, it took five years to find a publisher. After six rejections from various publishing houses, *The Mysterious Affair at Styles* – which introduced detective Hercule Poirot (whom she later described as 'insufferable') – was finally accepted by John Lane and published in 1920.

When Archibald revealed he was having an affair in 1926, Agatha disappeared, only to resurface 11 days later in the Swan Hydrophatic Hotel under an assumed name. There was talk of amnesia, a nervous breakdown, even a publicity hoax, although the truth was never revealed. Miss Marple popped up in a story in 1927, just before the couple's divorce.

The teetotal, non-smoking Christie married the archaeologist Max Mallowan in 1930, and her travels with him in the Middle East inspired several of her novels – *Murder on the Orient Express* was written in the Hotel Pera Palace in Istanbul.

In 1971, Christie was made a Dame Commander of the Order of the British Empire. Her health began to deteriorate and, towards the end of her life, she released two books for publication that had been sealed in a bank vault for over 30 years – *Curtain* and *Sleeping Murder*. She died in 1976, at the age of 85, in Wallingford, Oxfordshire. Her obituary in the *New York Times* was preceded by her fictional character Poirot, following his death in *Curtain* in 1975.

Barbara Cartland

The world's most prolific writer, Dame Barbara Cartland was born in Birmingham in 1901. Her father, a British Army officer, was killed on a Flanders battlefield, following which her mother opened a dress shop in London to make ends meet. Her brothers were killed in battle too, one day apart in 1940. Barbara spent a year as a gossip columnist for the *Daily Express*, where she was a favourite of Winston Churchill, before publishing her first novel, *Jigsaw*, in 1923. Popular in London society, and celebrated for her fashion sense, she married Alexander George McCorquodale, a former Army officer and heir to a British printing fortune in 1927, with whom she had one daughter, Raine, who would later become the stepmother of Diana, Princess of Wales. She obviously had a thing for the McCorquodales, because, after their divorce in 1936, Cartland married Alex's cousin Hugh. The Queen of Romance loved men, needless to say, and among her favourites were Sir Max Hastings and Lord Mountbatten, who was killed by the IRA in 1979.

Barbara wrote or dictated some 724 books, most of them romance novels, though she did pen *Barbara Cartland's Etiquette Handbook* and *How I Wish To Be Remembered* too, which was useful when it came to writing her obituary. Once, when asked by a famous Irish shrink if she thought the class system had been eroded she replied, 'Of course. Otherwise, do you really imagine I'd be sitting here talking to someone like you?'

Cartland was also famous for her involvement in charities and social causes and her pink chiffon outfits made her instantly recognisable. In 1992, she was named a Dame of the British Empire. She died on 21 May 2000, at the grand old age of 98.

Burns Supper

Every year, on 25 January, lovers of the Scottish poet Robert Burns come together to celebrate his life by eating haggis, drinking whisky and reading poems. Burns is the fellow responsible for writing 'Auld Lang Syne', the New Year anthem no one under 40 seems to know the words to. Robert Burns's cottage at Alloway, Ayrshire, was sold to a guild of shoemakers before his death and subsequently turned into an alehouse. It was here, in 1801, on the anniversary of his death, that the first recorded Burns Supper took place. A speech was made along with many toasts. Even the haggis was addressed, as well as a sheep's head (no longer customary fare, thankfully). Nine friends and patrons of Burns were present, among them one woman, although the suppers became mostly all-male affairs after that – until the late 20th century, that is. Celebrations were held twice a year until 1809, and thereafter on 25 January, as this fell in a slack period of the agricultural year.

John Keats wasn't impressed with what they'd done to Burns's home, complaining that the Alloway Inn degraded the poet's greatness. Paisley and Greenock were the first Burns Clubs, but by 1830 there were many throughout Scotland. The Ayr Festival of 1844 brought worldwide recognition of the celebration, while the Burns Federation, established in 1885, brought hundreds of clubs together. The first all-female club was founded at Shotts in Lanarkshire in 1920.

Charles Dickens

Charles Dickens is the quintessential Victorian writer. He was born in Portsmouth on 7 February 1812 and his family relocated to Camden in London when he was ten. He was fond of Henry Fielding's novels, and seems to have had a photographic memory. He attended William Giles's School in Chatham before his father was imprisoned for bad debt and the young Dickens had to be removed to work ten-hour days in Warren's Blacking Warehouse near Charing Cross Station, where he pasted labels on jars of shoe polish for six shillings a week. His time at the warehouse made him wretchedly miserable, and provided inspiration for his later novels *David Copperfield* and *Great Expectations*. Luckily, his father received a hefty inheritance and was released from debtors' prison, so Charles was able to return to school three years later.

Like so many great writers, his career began in journalism. Dickens landed jobs at *The Mirror of Parliament* and *The True Sun*, and at the age of 21 became a parliamentary journalist for *The Morning Chronicle*, where he wrote a series of sketches of London life under the pseudonym 'Boz'. Three years later, he married the editor's daughter, Catherine Hogarth, and within a month *Pickwick Papers* was published. Dickens didn't just write novels. There were autobiographies and travel books too, and he edited weekly periodicals like *Household Words* and *All Year Round*. He also wrote plays, performing before Queen Victoria in 1851. And on top of all this he managed to find the time to administer charitable organisations and to lecture against slavery in the United States, as well as fathering ten children and keeping a mistress. Little wonder he and his wife were estranged in 1858. He died in 1870 and his body rests at Westminster Cathedral.

English Language

Most of the Brits spoke a Celtic language before the Angles, Saxons and Jutes arrived from Denmark and Germany in the 5th century. From Englaland, the Angles spoke Englisc, so you can see where we got 'England' and 'English' from. This Old English, spoken up until around 1100, didn't sound anything like our language today, though around half the words we use have Old English roots. William the Conqueror, Duke of Normandy, invaded this isle in 1066 and brought French with him, though it was only spoken by the ruling elite, while the plebs carried on speaking English. By the 14th century, English was dominant again, though many French words had been added. Pronunciation shifted around the 15th century, with vowels being shortened, and now, with Britain having much wider contacts with the outside world, there were new influences on the language. The invention of printing was a huge step towards arriving at a common language, with standardised spelling and grammar. The dialect of London – the location of most publishing houses – became the standard towards the end of the 16th century, and the first English dictionary was published in 1604.

Oxford English Dictionary

The leading authority on the definition of words for over a century, the *Oxford English Dictionary* is a masterly work whose scholarship should not be taken for granted. In 1879, the Philological Society of London (who felt contemporary dictionaries were far from comprehensive) agreed with editor AH Murray and Oxford University Press to begin work on the *New English Dictionary*, with the aim of including all English language words from 1150 onwards. Murray and his team worked in the 'Scriptorium', in which they kept two tons of source quotations. They reckoned it would take ten years to complete, but five years into the project and they had only reached the diminutive 'ant'. Murray almost fell out with the Oxford Delegates on a number of occasions, and new editors joined the project until finally, in 1928, the last volume was completed and published. The new dictionary contained 400,000 entries. But the work didn't end there: as soon as the original was completed, the existing editors started work on updating it. In the early 1930s, the dictionary was reprinted in 12 volumes and was formally given its current title; a single-volume *Supplement* was also printed. Then in the 1980s Oxford University Press took on the mammoth task of creating an electronic text and a new updated second edition, with 5,000 new words. And the language keeps on growing …

Penguin Books

Britain's most recognisable publisher was founded in 1935 by Allen Lane. At the time, it was impossible to get your hands on quality fiction in paperback: you either had to fork out for a fancy hardback or visit the library. Lane was on his way back from visiting Agatha Christie in Devon when he found himself on a platform at Exeter Station without anything to read. All the bookstall had on offer were trashy Victorian novels and magazines. Lane, then a director of publisher Bodley Head, decided to produce quality paperbacks that would be as cheap as a pack of cigarettes and on sale alongside them everywhere, including railway stations. His secretary came up with the idea of a penguin as a symbol for the business, after Lane said he wanted something 'dignified but flippant'. An employee was duly sent to London Zoo to make some sketches, and the iconic logo was born.

The summer of 1935 saw the first Penguin paperbacks published by Bodley Head – among them Agatha Christie and Ernest Hemingway. They were colour-coded (orange for fiction, green for crime and blue for biography and non-fiction) and cost just sixpence. Penguin became a separate company in 1936, with premises in the Crypt of the Holy Trinity Church on Marylebone Road. They used a fairground slide to receive deliveries from the street above, and sold three million paperbacks within the first year alone. The world's first Penguincubator – a book dispenser – appeared on Charing Cross Road in 1937.

Poet Laureate

Poets have been singing for their supper in the royal court since the time of Richard the Lionheart. Back in the 1300s, Geoffrey Chaucer was a *'Versificator Regis'*, paid annually in wine, and Ben Jonson also received an annual 'terse of Canary wine'. But it was only in 1668, when John Dryden was appointed by James II (before subsequently being sacked by William III), that the laureateship became an official post attached to the royal household. The Poet Laureate was responsible for writing occasional poems on royal births, marriages and deaths, as well as important public events. Some of the greatest English poets have been Poet Laureate: John Dryden, Alfred Lord Tennyson (whose most famous poem was 'The Charge of the Light Brigade') and William Wordsworth (who famously didn't write a single poem throughout his long laureateship). Some of the cuddliest English poets – namely John Betjeman – have also been Laureate.

Officially, the Laureate is appointed by the Lord Chamberlain on behalf of the monarch, but in reality the prime minister and his or her advisers have been making the choice for the past 200 years. There's no job description, and the salary is small. It used to be a job for life until 1999, when Andrew Motion was appointed for a fixed term of ten years. Motion later said, 'The job has been incredibly difficult and entirely thankless.' Hopefully the recently appointed Carol Ann Duffy, the first lady laureate, won't find it all such a bore.

The Romantics

While the rest of the country was busy with the industrialisation and urbanisation of Britain from the late 18th century onwards, a bunch of poets – namely Blake, Wordsworth, Coleridge, Byron, Shelley and Keats – were wandering around, dreaming up pretty ways of expressing their innermost feelings. With the French Revolution fresh in their minds, they were partly reacting against the reductive rationalisation that had gripped the country. Big emotions were key, and nature was their guide and goddess. Wordsworth practised what he preached, wandering lonely as a cloud up in the Lake District, while Coleridge drenched his poetry in opium-induced imagery. Byron shocked the world with his wild affairs, becoming a cult figure while still alive; Shelley's poetry was obscure, his attitude atheist, marking the founding of a new, more difficult, modernist poetry; while Keats's poetry was itself a substitute for religion. Their early deaths sealed their reputations and encouraged the notion of suffering for one's art, the loneliness of the genius poet. They must have turned in their graves in the 1980s, when the New Romantic wave hit the UK, with the likes of Adam and the Ants and Spandau Ballet mincing about in frilly blouses.

Shakespeare

It's hard to believe that the greatest playwright the world has ever known only lived for 52 years. Born in Stratford-upon-Avon on 26 April 1564 to a glovemaker and a local landowner's daughter, he probably attended Stratford's grammar school. I say 'probably' because not much is known about his life. At 18, he married Anne Hathaway, with whom he had a daughter Susanna, and twins Judith and Hamnet (who died aged 11). Less than ten years later, he was working as an actor and writer with the Lord Chamberlain's Company, later to become the King's Company, in London. They ran two theatres around Southwark, near the Thames – the Globe and the Blackfriars. Two of Shakespeare's poems appeared in print in 1593 and 1594, and from then onwards he penned two plays a year. Some of the earliest works include *A Midsummer Night's Dream* and *The Merchant of Venice*. The tragedies – *Hamlet, King Lear, Macbeth* – came later. From 1608 until his death, William was writing tragicomedies such as *The Tempest*.

Shakespeare retired to Stratford a wealthy man, and died on 23 April 1616. The Bard (meaning professional poet) wrote 38 plays and 154 sonnets, as well as several other poems. Almost 400 years after Shakespeare's death, we're still speculating on the colour of his eyes, his religious beliefs, even his sexual preferences. A modern reconstruction of the Globe Theatre, founded by Shakespeare, was opened in 1997 on the South Bank of the River Thames.

Sherlock Holmes

With his deerstalker hat and pipe, Detective Sherlock Holmes is one of the world's most recognisable fictional sleuths. His creator, Arthur Conan Doyle, born in Edinburgh in 1859, trained as a doctor. In his time he worked on board an Arctic whaler, was a war correspondent in Egypt and stood (unsuccessfully) for Parliament. Holmes first appeared in the 1887 novel *A Study in Scarlet*, for which Conan Doyle was paid £25. A series of serialised Holmes novels and stories followed in *The Strand Magazine*, but after a few years Conan Doyle felt the detective was keeping the author's mind 'from better things'. Accordingly, Doyle killed Holmes off in his 1893 book 'The Final Problem', in *The Memoirs of Sherlock Holmes* — Holmes's arch-enemy Moriarty throw him to his death from the top of Reichenbach Falls in Switzerland. Readers were so distraught, however, that the author was prevailed upon to bring Holmes back from the dead. In 'The Adventure of the Empty House', in *The Return of Sherlock Holmes*, readers were delighted to discover that Holmes had, in fact, survived the fight at Reichenbach Falls, and had rock-climbed back up the cliff. Holmes retired to a bee farm on the Sussex Downs in 1903 and wrote *A Practical Handbook of Bee Culture, with some Observations upon the Segregation of the Queen*.

All in all, four novels and 56 short stories featuring Holmes were written. Almost all were narrated by the detective's friend and biographer, Dr John H Watson, who disapproved of the detective's addiction to cocaine and morphine (both legal drugs in the 19th century).

CHAPTER TWELVE
KIDS' STUFF

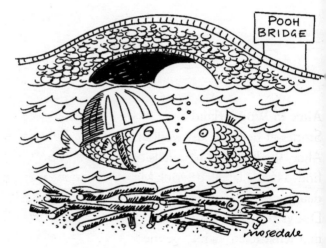

'I'm not taking any chances this time.'

KIDS' STUFF

Alice in Wonderland

Stories at bedtime just wouldn't be the same without Alice, the little girl who falls down a rabbit hole and finds a bottle labelled 'Drink Me'. Alice Liddell was the daughter of a friend of one Reverend Charles Dodgson, the Anglican priest and Oxford mathematician who penned *Alice's Adventures in Wonderland* in 1865. Inspiration for the story struck one balmy July afternoon, when the reverend, along with a colleague and his three young daughters – Alice among them – was rowing down the River Isis to Godstow. 'Many a day we rowed together on that quiet stream – the three little maidens and I – and many a fairy tale had been extemporised for their benefit – yet none of these tales got written down: they lived and died, like summer midges, each in its own golden afternoon until there came a day when, as it chanced, one of the listeners petitioned that the tale might be written down for her,' Alice's father wrote later. That story was *Alice's Adventures Underground*.

Alice herself recalled, 'Sometimes to tease us, Mr Dodgson would stop and say suddenly, "That's all till next time."

'"Oh," we would cry, "it's not bedtime already!" and he would go on. Another time the story would begin in the boat and Mr Dodgson would pretend to fall asleep in the middle, to our great dismay.'

Dodgson presented Alice with a hand-printed edition of the book, illustrated with 37 of his own drawings, for Christmas 1864. His friends urged him to have it published, so the following year, after some revision and expansion, *Alice's Adventures in Wonderland* appeared, under the nom de plume Lewis Carroll, since Dodgson had a professional reputation to uphold. Sales were astonishing, and the book became a publishing sensation. Queen Victoria and Oscar Wilde were fans, and before long Carroll was hard at work on *Through the Looking-Glass, and What Alice Found There*, which was published in 1971 and was even more successful.

Beatrix Potter

The woman who created Peter Rabbit led a secluded life as a child, and was taught at home in South Kensington by a series of governesses. Beatrix had many pets, among them a rabbit – Peter – which she took everywhere on a lead. In 1893, at the age of 27, she wrote and illustrated *The Tale of Peter Rabbit* and posted it to her last governess's sickly five-year-old child. Encouraged by the governess, Beatrix printed 250 copies in 1901, just in time for Christmas. They sold very quickly and had to be reprinted a few weeks later. Frederick Warne & Co. printed 8,000 copies the following year, and it's never been out of print since.

Potter became secretly engaged to Norman Warne in 1905, as her parents didn't approve of her marrying a common tradesman, but soon afterwards he died of pernicious anaemia. Beatrix wrote in a letter to her sister, 'I must try to make a fresh beginning next year.' She bought Hill Top Farm in the Lake District and went on to publish 22 books over the next 28 years, as well as farming and breeding Hardwick sheep. Having married a local solicitor when in her mid-forties, Beatrix purchased 15 farms and over 4,000 acres of land. The couple adopted a pet hedgehog and called her Mrs

Tiggywinkle; the creature's spiky ways inspired *The Tale of Mrs Tiggywinkle*, published in 1905. Potter was a lifelong nature lover and, following her death in 1943, her land was left to the National Trust to help to maintain the unspoiled nature of the Lake District.

Enid Blyton

A quintessentially British children's storyteller, the author of the Famous Five, Secret Seven and Noddy books was born above a shop in London's East Dulwich in 1897. Blyton (also known as Mary Pollock) was very close to her father, who encouraged her interests in nature, music, art and literature. Among her favourite books were *Little Women* and *Black Beauty*, and Enid took to writing compulsively after her parents' marriage broke up when she was just 13 – but her mother referred to her 'scribblings' as a 'waste of time'. Fortunately, she continued undeterred. She was also musically gifted, but she turned down a place at the Guildhall School of Music in favour of teaching.

Blyton's first book was a collection of poems called *Child Whispers*, and was published in 1922. She married Major Hugh Alexander Pollock in 1924, an editor she'd met when she was commissioned to write a book about London Zoo. She wrote and edited a weekly magazine called *Sunny Stories for Little Folks* and her first full-length book, *The Enid Blyton Book of Bunnies*, was published in 1925. Blyton remarried – to a surgeon called Kenneth Darrell Waters – in 1943. By 1950, she had earned a fortune through her writing, and set up her own publishing company, Darrell Waters Ltd. After a battle with Alzheimer's, Blyton died in a nursing home in Hampstead on 28 November 1968, aged 71.

Enid Blyton wrote around 700 books and, despite criticisms of political incorrectness, they have sold over 400 million copies to date, still selling over a million a year. Over 3,400 of her books are available in translation (ranking just behind Shakespeare).

Harry Potter

It's hard to imagine life without Harry Potter, the world's most famous little wizard. In 1990, Joanne Rowling, who had been writing since the age of six, was on a train from Manchester to London, when the idea for Harry suddenly came to her – though the author says she had no idea where from. When she arrived at Clapham Junction, she began writing immediately. Rowling was working for Amnesty International at the time, and moved to Portugal shortly afterwards to teach English as a foreign language. There she married a journalist, with whom she had one child. The marriage quickly broke down and she and her daughter moved back to Edinburgh to be near Rowling's sister. Somehow, as a single mum on social welfare – and recently diagnosed with clinical depression – she managed to complete her first novel, *Harry Potter and the Philosopher's Stone*, which she wrote by hand in Edinburgh cafés.

In 1995, the agent Christopher Little agreed to take her on and, after the manuscript had been rejected by eight other publishers, Bloomsbury offered her an advance on publication of £2,500. Her publishers thought it would be a good idea to adopt a more gender-neutral pseudonym for her male readers, hence the name JK Rowling. The book was released in the UK on 30 June 1997. Rowling received $105,000 for the American rights, an unprecedented amount for an unknown children's author.

The series of Harry Potter books, numbering seven in total, is now a global brand worth an estimated £7 billion and the last four Harry Potter titles have set records as the fastest-selling books in history. That, along with the success of the movie spin-offs, has made JK Rowling very comfortable indeed – the 2008 *Sunday Times* Rich List placed her as the 144th richest person in Britain, and the 12th richest woman. Harry might not have a share in his creator's fortunes, but they do share the same birthday – 31st July – as does Danielle Radcliffe, the actor who plays Harry on the big screen.

Ladybird Books

A Loughborough printer by the name of Wills and Hepworth produced the first Ladybird book during the First World War and registered the logo in 1915. The company's aim was to publish 'pure and healthy literature' for children, although their first efforts were a bit wide of the mark: their *ABC Picture Book* featured armoured trains for the letter A. The hardback pocket-sized books that we know and love were first published in 1940, with *Bunnikin's Picnic Party*. They cost only half a crown, and stayed that way for 30 years.

In the 1960s, William Murray discovered that just 12 words make up 25 per cent of the words we speak. Based on this, a new Key Words Reading Scheme – better known as the 'Peter and Jane' books – was introduced in 1964. Murray, a former teacher who wrote the original books in the series, proclaimed learning to read was like 'falling off a log'. It is rumoured that Ladybird's *How it Works: The*

Motor Car was used by Thames Valley Police driving school in the 1960s. And *How it Works: The Computer* was used by university lecturers, as well as by the Ministry of Defence, although they had their books covered in brown paper to save face.

Mr Men

There's a Mr Man or Little Miss just bursting to get out of every one of us, whether it's a Mr Messy or Little Miss Naughty. Creator of the characters Roger Hargreaves was born in Yorkshire in 1935 and worked as an advertising copy writer for 20 years, working on campaigns for Lindt chocolate and Pimms among others. One morning over breakfast, his young son Adam asked, 'What does a tickle look like?' and Roger drew a little orange man with unfeasibly long arms. And so it was that Mr Tickle was born. Hargreaves went on to write six books – about Mr Tickle, Mr Greedy, Mr Happy, Mr Nosey, Mr Sneeze and Mr Bump – but struggled to find a publisher for them. When he did finally stumble upon one, the books became an instant success, selling more than a million copies in the first three years alone. Hargreaves gave up his office job the following year, and the first Little Miss book appeared in 1981. Roger died in 1988, but his son

Adam, who had asked the original million-dollar question, took up the pen.

Paddington Bear

Paddington first appeared with his old hat, battered suitcase and penchant for marmalade sandwiches on 13 October 1958. His creator, Michael Bond, was inspired to write about him after he noticed a lone teddy bear in a store near Paddington Station on Christmas Eve, which he bought as a present for his wife. The little bear inspired Bond to pen a story about a furry stowaway from darkest Peru, and within ten days *A Bear Called Paddington* was complete. Bond had the image of child evacuees of the Second World War in mind when he wrote about a bear – with a note attached to him which reads 'Please look after this bear. Thank you.' – who was found by the Brown family in Paddington Station. Paddington then lives with the Browns, at 32 Windsor Gardens, off the Harrow Road.

Bond had wanted him to come from 'darkest Africa' but his agent informed him there weren't any bears there. The author said of his marmalade-sandwich-eating character, 'The great advantage of having a bear as a central character is that he can combine the innocence of a child with the sophistication of an adult. Paddington is not the sort of bear that would ever go to the moon – he has his paws too firmly on the ground for that. He gets involved in everyday situations.'

Perhaps this explains why over 35 million copies of the Paddington books have sold.

Peter Pan

By the end of the 1800s, 37-year-old Scottish novelist and playwright James Matthew Barrie was famous on both sides of the pond, with fans that included Henry James and Robert Louis Stevenson. He met a Mrs Davies, 'the most beautiful creature he had ever seen', at a New Year's party in 1897 and went on to spend a great deal of time with her and her husband and five children, finding inspiration to write about 'a lost childhood'. Peter Pan first appeared in a section of *The Little White Bird*, a 1902 novel written for adults, with the play *Peter Pan, or The Boy Who Wouldn't Grow Up* debuting at the Duke of York Theatre two years later. His publishers extracted the few chapters from the novel in which Peter Pan appeared and republished them in 1906 as *Peter Pan in Kensington Gardens*. 'I made Peter by rubbing the five of you violently together, as savages with two sticks produce a flame,' Barrie later told the Davies children.

Barrie gave all the rights to the story to Great Ormond Street Hospital in 1929, claiming that Peter Pan had been a patient there and that 'It was he who put me up to the little thing I did for the hospital.' He even organised a production at the hospital, in which he himself played Peter Pan.

On 6 April 1960, the *New York Times* announced 'Barrie's Peter Pan Killed by a London Subway Train'. Sadly, Peter Davies, one of the children who had inspired the 'boy who wouldn't grow up', had taken his own life.

Poohsticks

For those of you who haven't played this delightful game before, it's pretty simple: standing on a bridge, competitors drop sticks into the river upstream and see which one reaches the other side of the bridge first. The man who came up with the game is none other than AA Milne of Winnie-the-Pooh fame. It first appears in *The House at Pooh* Corner, and the bridge featured in the book is modelled on the footbridge across a tributary of the River Medway near the Milnes' home. The annual World Poohsticks Championships are held every year at Day's Lock on the River Thames.

Postman Pat

Postman Pat and his black-and-white cat have been on TV since 1981. John Cunliffe is the man who dreamed him up while living in Kendal in the Lake District. He used to chat to a fellow who ran the little post office at the end of his street and from their conversations learned how postmen went about their work. Later, while teaching at Castle Park School, a colleague took Cunliffe around the local farms to familiarise him with their simple, rural way of life. One of his students' parents told him that the BBC were looking for writers for a new TV series, so Cunliffe set about writing the first Postman Pat episode, basing the village of Greendale, with its winding roads and sheep, on the real-life village of Longsleddale in Cumbria.

Punch and Judy

A puppet show featuring an infanticidal, wife-beating psychopath and his beaten wife, Punch and Judy can be traced back to the *commedia dell'arte* of 16th-century Italy, an improvised open-air theatre. Punch is based on the character Pulcinella, the pagan Lord of Misrule who presided over the Feast of Fools, in Neapolitan puppetry. His wife was originally called the less glamorous 'Joan'. On 9 May

1662, the diarist Samuel Pepys recounted seeing an 'Italian puppet play' in Covent Garden, and this was Punch's earliest known appearance on these shores. Punch enjoyed the limelight throughout the 18th century, in Covent Garden and Bath in particular. Even Henry Fielding ran his own puppet theatre, under the pseudonym Madame de la Nash.

Marionette shows, which were expensive and cumbersome to produce, were replaced in the latter half of the 18th century by glove-puppet shows, performed by one puppeteer – known since the 19th century as a 'professor' – from within the familiar narrow booth, with an assistant 'bottler' to pass around the hat. Around this time, Punch became more unhinged and violent. No one knows quite why, but ironically it was around this time that Punch and Judy evolved into children's entertainment and Punch's exultant cry of 'That's the way to do it' was heard in seaside resorts across the UK.

Roald Dahl

Roald Dahl was born to Norwegian parents in Llandaff in Wales in 1916. When he was just three years old, he lost his eldest sister to appendicitis, and his father just a couple of months later to pneumonia. Although Roald wasn't fond of school, he was lucky enough to become a tester for Cadbury's chocolate. He joined Shell Petroleum in July 1934 and worked in Tanzania, before joining the Royal Air Force in Nairobi in 1939, and narrowly escaped with his life in 1940 after a crash landing. His first piece of writing 'Shot Down Over Libya' was published in the American *Saturday Evening Post* in 1942. Dahl married Patricia Neal in New York in 1953 and they moved back to England. His first children's book was *The Gremlins*, commissioned by Walt Disney for a film that was never made and published in 1943. He went on to create some of the best-loved children's stories of the 20th century, including *Charlie and the Chocolate Factory* and *James and the Giant Peach*. He also wrote macabre adult stories, and later it emerged that he had been an agent for MI6, working closely with Ian Fleming, creator of James Bond. He died at the age of 74 and was buried with snooker cues, some very good burgundy, chocolates and HB pencils.

Winnie-the-Pooh

Pooh Bear was created by AA Milne, who was born in Kilburn, London, in 1882. He was an assistant editor at *Punch* magazine, wrote 18 plays and three novels and served as an officer in the First World

War and Captain of the Home Guard in the Second. He married in 1913 and his only son, Christopher Robin Milne, was born seven years later. The poem 'Teddy Bear', featuring his son's teddy Edward, first appeared in *Punch* in 1923, and then again in his collection *When We Were Very Young* a year later, which also introduced us to Christopher Robin as narrator. The bear had morphed into Winnie-the-Pooh by Christmas 1925, when he appeared in a story commissioned by the *Evening News*. He had been renamed by Christopher after a Canadian black bear called Winnie in London Zoo, while Pooh was a swan they'd met on a family holiday. The *Punch* illustrator, EH Shephard, fashioned the bear after his son's teddy, named Growler. *Winnie-the-Pooh* was published by Methuen in 1926, followed by *The House at Pooh Corner* in 1928. A second collection of nursery rhymes, *Now We Are Six*, was also published in 1927. The Hundred Acre Wood featured in the Pooh books was based on the Five Hundred Acre Wood near the Milnes' home in East Sussex.

Stephen Slesinger purchased US merchandising and television rights to the bear in 1930 and by 1931 Pooh was a $50 million-a-year business, with Disney taking him over in 1961.

CHAPTER THIRTEEN
ODDS & ENDS

'Well thank God...I thought for a minute you were a kissogram.'

ODDS & ENDS

Allotments

Rented out for individuals to grown their own fruits and vegetables, these beloved lots of land date back to the 1500s, when land was stripped from the poor by the Church and aristocracy, and replaced by tiny allotments attached to their tenant cottages. Fearing civil unrest, the General Enclosure Act of 1845 meant that, although rich landowners could still stop the poor grazing their animals on common land, they had to provide 'field gardens', limited to a quarter of an acre, as compensation. The 19th century saw mass migration to the cities, and with it what the Victorians referred to as 'degeneracy' among the poor: allotments offered a healthy distraction from boozing.

As housing proliferated and gardens grew smaller, the urban allotment became more commonplace. During the First World War, the number of allotments doubled to 1.5 million, one notable area of growth being along railway lines. Rationing throughout the Second World War and up until 1954 meant that they became an even more important source of food, and even public parks were used for cultivation of food. 'Dig for Victory' posters were everywhere, and they seemed to do the trick, as each allotment produced almost a tonne of fruit and veg each year. Today there are fewer than 250,000 allotments. For most city dwellers, it seems, a window box will do.

Boxing Day

One would be hard-pressed to find a soul in England who doesn't know that Boxing Day is the day after Christmas Day, but, if you think Boxing Day has something to do with our sporting past, think again. In 17th-century Britain, it was common at Christmas for apprentices to carry around ceramic boxes – named Christmas boxes – in case their masters' customers were kind enough to offer seasonal gifts of money. The cash would then be shared among everyone in the company as an end-of-year bonus.

A century on, the term Christmas Box had lost its specific meaning and come to represent any financial gift bequeathed by a member of the public to tradesmen, postmen, milkmen and the like to thank them and wish them season's greetings. Over the next hundred years, it became more and more customary for public-service employees (and, increasingly, anyone who felt like asking) to request financial donations by knocking on doors or merely approaching people in the street on the day after Christmas. Presumably, the logic was that, of all the days of the year, this day (when so much giving had been done) would see many people laden with unwanted gifts, or with guilt about their good fortunes, and that they would be only too happy to be unburdened of either. Hence, in the 18th century, the day became known as Boxing Day.

British Bulldog

This barrel-chested, loose-skinned, flat-headed canine has come to symbolise Britain. As Winston Churchill put it, 'The nose of the bulldog has been slanted backwards so he can breathe without letting go,' suggesting the great resolve of the British people. Incidentally, because of these stunted airways, bulldogs snore very badly. The term 'bulldog' was first used in the late 16th century. It is thought that bulldogs were bred in England as a cross between the mastiff and the pug, although this is still hotly contested. Back in the 17th century, the bulldog was bred for bullbaiting, a popular gambling blood sport, which was performed twice a week at Hockley-in-the-Hole in London, and in provincial towns throughout the UK. It typically involved a bull being tethered to a pole in a ring (sometimes with pepper blown up its nose to really get it going) with specially trained dogs being set on it, one by one, to try to put it out of action. One of the bulldog's methods of immobilisation was to latch on to the animal's snout (that's where the slanted nose came in – and the folds in his face meant that the bull's blood wouldn't drip into his eyes). It was believed that the meat would be more tender and nutritious if it had been baited before slaughter. Indeed, butchers who sold meat that hadn't been baited were liable to a penalty. This practice was banned, however, by the Cruelty to Animals Act in 1835, causing a huge outcry at the time about the 'death of a traditional sport'. The number of pure-bred bulldogs quickly declined.

Garden Shed

Traditionally a retreat from domestic life, the garden shed, in its many guises as a storeroom, a workshop, a retreat, a haven of peace and quiet, and even an illicit meeting place, has been with us for some 600 years or more. A multi-functionary wooden structure, commonly found in back gardens and allotments, the shed derives its name from the Old English word 'sceadu', meaning shade, shadow or darkness, which seems appropriate, as many's the man who has tripped over his lawnmower in the dark of night. The shed was first mentioned in 1481 by the printer William Caxton, who described, 'A yerde in which was a shadde where in were five grete dogges.' The garden shed we know and love evolved in the 1920s and 1930s with the growth of the suburbs, with their crazy paving, birdbaths and pergolas. The first National Shed Week was held in the UK in 2007. Winners thus far have included a shed converted into a Roman Temple and a 'Pub Shed'.

Loch Ness Monster

No one's ever proved that she exists, but this hasn't stopped thousands of diehard Nessie-watchers wanting to believe. And they've been believing for many a century. The earliest mention of the creature is recorded in the 7th-century *Life of St Columba* by Adomnan. Guilty for being partly responsible for the death of many men in the Battle of Cul-drebene, St Columba set out to mainland Scotland on a pilgrimage to spread Christianity across the land. He ran into some Picts on his travels, and noticed they were burying a man. Apparently, he had been savaged by a 'water beast', and dragged under water near the loch. The men had only been able to recover a dead body. The story goes that Columba astonished his new Pict pals by instructing one of his followers to swim across the River Ness. The beast soon made a move to attack, but Columba quickly made the sign of the cross and ordered the monster to 'Go no further'. The monster did as it was told, did an about-turn and beat a hasty retreat. This tale was proof enough for many, but it was a sighting many centuries later that really brought Nessie on to the world stage.

In 1933, the *Inverness Courier* carried a report written by the water bailiff for Loch Ness claiming that a London man by the name of George Spicer had seen 'the nearest approach to a dragon or prehistoric animal that I have ever seen in my life' crossing the road near the loch carrying 'an animal' in its mouth. Other stories came flooding in to the

Courier of a 'monster fish', a 'sea serpent' and a 'dragon'. Nessie had her first official photograph taken in 1933. The Secretary of Scotland stepped in at this stage – not to tell everyone they were mad but to order the police to protect the poor creature from attack. The picture later turned out to be a hoax. One of the most recognisable images of Nessie is the 'Surgeon's Photograph', taken by a London gynaecologist and published in the *Daily Mail* in 1934, featuring the head and neck of the old girl. It was also revealed to be a hoax.

Since then, there have been multiple dubious reports of the monster – photos, videos, sonar readings – and the relentless pursuit of Nessie goes on, fuelled by the nation's fascination and the gruelling determination of a few obsessives. The last sighting was in 2007 by Gordon Holmes who produced video footage of a 'jet black thing, about 45 feet long, moving fairly fast in the water'. It has been suggested the subject of his video may well be an otter.

Pillar Box

Back in the 1600s, the only letters delivered were those to and from the King, but by 1635 the use of Royal Mail had been extended to the public. At first, it was customary for the recipient to pay for their own letter, and it was only in 1680 that the penny post was introduced, and the sender could pay his postage in advance. For years, anyone wanting to post a letter had to travel to a Post Office, but the advent of post boxes changed all that.

In 1840, the Uniform Penny Post was introduced in the UK, and could be paid for with the world's first postage stamp, the Penny Black. It may come as a surprise, but the man who brought us one of the UK's most recognisable items of street furniture – the bright-red post box – is none other than the prolific novelist Anthony Trollope. Trollope was a surveyor's clerk for the Post Office in Britain and Ireland for over 30 years (sometimes dipping into the 'lost letter' box for ideas for his novels) and introduced the pillar box in 1852, the first of which appeared at St Helier in Jersey. In 1853, the first British mainland pillar box was erected at Botchergate in Carlisle. A similar box from the same year still stands at Barnes Cross, Bishop's Caundle in Dorset, the oldest pillar box still in use on the mainland.

In 1856, Richard Redgrave of the Department of Science and Art designed an ornate bronze pillar box for use in London and other large cities, an example of which can be found at the Victoria and

Albert Museum. A less ornate version was used in other towns and cities, and in 1859 the box design was improved by moving the aperture from the top to below the rim and thus the first National Standard pillar box was born – and it was green.

The red colour was adopted from 1874 onwards, when repainting of London boxes began. It took ten years to finish the job.

Incidentally, the earliest form of postcode was introduced in London in 1857, dividing London into districts denoted by compass points: 'N' for north, 'S' for south and so on. Numbers were added to divide them up more specifically into NW1, SW2, etc. in 1916 during the First World War.

Red Telephone Box

You can't miss these red kiosks, with their domed roofs and crown insignias, which were once in every town across the UK, Malta, Bermuda and Gibraltar. The first telephone box was introduced in 1920, but did not resemble the red boxes we all know and love. The box was designed in 1935 by Giles Gilbert Scott – who also designed Waterloo Bridge, Battersea Power Station and the Tate Modern building – to coincide with the Jubilee of King George V. Sadly the King did not live to see any such examples installed, but prototype of Scott's design – the K6 model (K for Kiosk) – still stands in the entrance to the Royal Academy. Scott had suggested a silver exterior and a 'greeny-blue' interior but the Post Office chose to paint it red to make it more conspicuous.

In 1952 'Elizabethan' crowned examples were introduced. Two years later, it was noted that Queen Elizabeth II was not the second Queen of Scotland, thus modifications to the K6 were required. Interchangeable crowns were cast so that kiosks destined for 'North of the border' could sport the Scottish crown.

British Telecom began replacing the red box with a more utilitarian model in 1996 – the KX 1100 PLUS. There are still over 14,000 K6 boxes in operation, each of which costs £2,000 a year to maintain.

The Ministry of Magic – the institution for wizards in the country in the Harry Potter books – is located in the London underground and is accessed via one of these much-loved telephone boxes.

Stiff Upper Lip

The stiff upper lip is not a physical characteristic of the British; rather it refers to the reserved nature of its people, who (in theory, at any rate) keep their emotions in check and never betray any weakness, even in the face of great adversity. We may consider keeping a stiff upper lip to be very British, but the phrase was coined by the Americans, with its first recorded usage in 1815 in the Boston newspaper the *Massachusetts Spy*. But times are changing, it seems. Look around these days and you're more likely to find the trembling lower lip. If you want to watch a load of post-war Brits letting it all hang out, a good starting point would be British reality TV, where shameless histrionics from celebs and wannabes who should know better are in plentiful supply.

Toby Jugs

Fashioned in the shape of a heavy-set jolly old fellow holding a mug of beer in one hand and a pipe in the other, these ceramic mugs first became popular in the 1760s. They were produced by the Staffordshire potters and may have been based on similar Delft jugs made in the Netherlands. The name most likely comes from a notorious Yorkshire drinker by the name of Henry Elwes, known to his friends as 'Toby Fillpot', for whom the old drinking song 'The Brown Jug' was written. Toby Jugs are also known as Fillpots, so that would make sense. These jugs would have been used for drinking, of course, and would sometimes feature caricatures of famous politicians, although nowadays they're mostly ornamental. Very tasteful too.

Union Jack

The Union Flag, commonly known as the Union Jack, is the national flag of the United Kingdom. Its current design, dating back to 1801, incorporates the flags of St George (England's patron saint) and St Andrew (Scotland's patron saint) and the cross of St Patrick (Ireland's patron saint). Wales isn't included, as it was already legally part of the Kingdom of England. The first step in the creation of the Union Flag was back in 1606, when King James VI of Scotland became King of England. It proved unpopular, though, as the English resented the background being blue (and thus Scottish), while the Scottish resented the red cross being superimposed on the Scottish white cross.

It is a criminal offence to fly the Union Jack from a non-naval/military ship at sea. Australia, New Zealand, Tuvalu and Fiji, as well as many other former British colonies, incorporate the Union Jack into their national flags. A campaign was started in 2003 to put some black in the Union Jack, but it was deemed 'ridiculous tokenism' that would 'do nothing to stamp out racism'.

While the flag has often been associated with right-wing sympathies, in recent years it has come to symbolise 'Cool Britannia' and can be found emblazoned on everything from condoms to contact lenses. Its popularity reached a pinnacle in 1997 when the Spice Girls' Geri Haliwell wore a Union Jack dress to the BRIT Awards.

Watershed

You can't see, hear or smell it, but the watershed is nonetheless an integral part of the British psyche. It is television's dividing line between good and evil. A watershed is something that separates one era from another, or a historically significant event that causes or marks great change. The literal meaning is the separation of a river or waterway, from the German *wasserscheide*. The watershed in the UK is 9pm. In other words, it's OK to show TV programmes with 'adult content', i.e. sex and violence, after 9pm and before 5.30am. Some 12+ shows, such as *The Simpsons*, can be shown before 9pm, while subscription services such as Sky Movies are free from such constraints. The Office of Communications (Ofcom) is the controlling regulatory body. The unofficial controlling body for many years was morality campaigner Mary Whitehouse.

INDEX